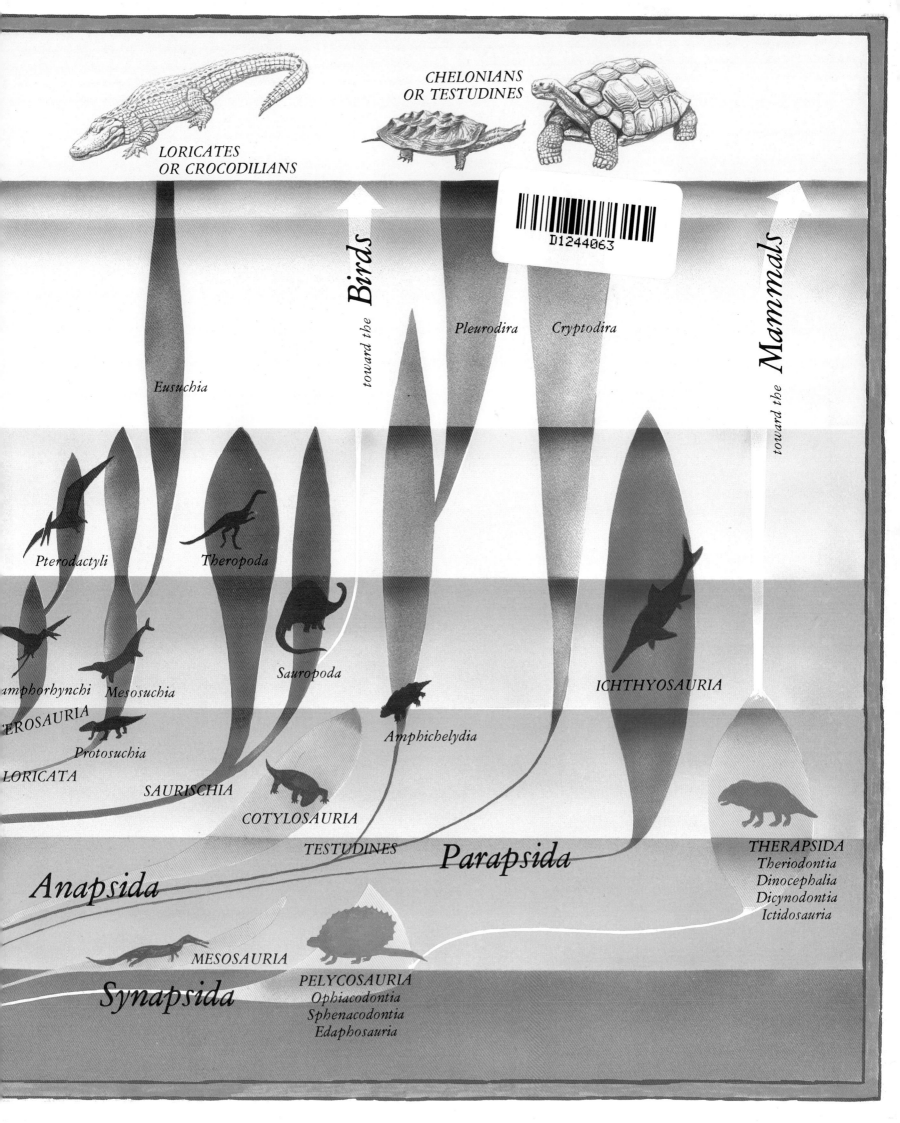

LORICATES
OR CROCODILIANS

CHELONIANS
OR TESTUDINES

toward the Birds

toward the Mammals

Eusuchia

Pleurodira

Cryptodira

Pterodactyli

Theropoda

amphorhynchi   *Mesosuchia*

Sauropoda

ICHTHYOSAURIA

'EROSAURIA

Protosuchia

Amphichelydia

LORICATA

SAURISCHIA

COTYLOSAURIA

THERAPSIDA
Theriodontia
Dinocephalia
Dicynodontia
Ictidosauria

TESTUDINES

Parapsida

Anapsida

MESOSAURIA

PELYCOSAURIA
Ophiacodontia
Sphenacodontia
Edaphosauria

Synapsida

THE HISTORY OF LIFE ON EARTH

REPTILES

editorial coordination
CATERINA LONGANESI

CONTENTS

Library of Congress Cataloging-in-Publication Data

Minelli, Giuseppe.
  Reptiles.

  (The History of life on earth)
  Translation and adaptation of: I rettili.
  Summary: Describes the physical characteristics of reptiles and traces their evolutionary history from 300 million years ago to the present.
  1. Reptiles—Evolution—Juvenile literature.
2. Reptiles, Fossil—Juvenile literature. [1. Reptiles.
2. Reptiles, Fossil] I. Minelli, G. Rettili. English.
II. Orlandi, Lorenzo. III. Title. IV. Series.
QL665.F59 1987 597.9 86-32905
ISBN 0-8160-1558-9

color separation by
Carlo Scotti, Milan
photosetting by
Elle Due, Milan
printed and bound in Italy by
Tipolitografia G. Canale & C. Spa, Turin

REPTILES

Giuseppe Minelli

Professor of Comparative Anatomy
University of Bologna, Italy

illustrated by
Lorenzo Orlandi

translated and adapted by
Bryan Fleming

the "History of Life on Earth" series
is conceived, designed and produced by
Jaca Book

Facts On File Publications
New York, New York ● Oxford, England

Dimorphodon
flying reptile

Monitor
saurian

Kentrurosaurus
dinosaur

Camptosaurus
mesosaur

Eurasia

LAURASIA

Triceratops
dinosaur

North
America

Turtle
chelonian

PANGAEA

Equator

PANTHALASSA

PANTHALASSA

Africa

Tuatara
rhynchocephalian

South
America

GONDWANALAND

India

Australia

Iguanodon
dinosaur

Antarctic

Megalosaurus
dinosaur

Snake
ophidian

Crocodile
loricate

Brachiosaurus
dinosaur

During the Secondary Era, 225 million years ago, all the land on the Earth formed one single supercontinent, Pangaea, surrounded by one single ocean, Panthalassa. About 130 million years ago, owing to the continental drift, the northern mass of land, called Laurasia, detached itself from the southern one, called Gondwanaland, along the equator. Practically all the land above sea level was dominated by reptiles. There were many of them, especially dinosaurs, and they flourished particularly in the Jurassic-Cretaceous Period. For some mysterious reason, they became almost totally extinct at the end of that period, some 65 million years ago.

1. THE REPTILE

A SLANDERED ANIMAL

Many are the words that have a sinister aura, that call frightening pictures to mind. They are handed down in literature and in popular sayings. The word "reptile" is one of them. It comes from the Latin term "reptilis," meaning "creeping," and it is used to express lowliness, insincerity, and hidden, lurking danger, because the reptile, in our minds, is usually a slithery creepy-crawly, ready to snap and attack without warning. This book is not intended to change all that, but what it will do is to try and give its due to a large class of vertebrates that were the protagonists of extraordinary, fascinating events. First of all, reptiles are *not* slithery: their skin is always dry, sometimes rough and creased, such as in crocodiles, turtles, and tortoises; sometimes smooth and delicate, such as in

snakes. Besides, if it is true that many reptiles do creep, it is equally true that the snakes are a minority compared to the reptiles that move about in other ways, often even with elegance and grace. But there are far more important, and better substantiated, reasons for the glory of the reptiles.

THE FIRST REAL TERRESTRIAL VERTEBRATES

The reptiles were the first vertebrates that were able to shake themselves free from the slavery of their water habitat and also go off to live and reproduce on the land above sea level, in drier environments. This was by no means an unimportant event; on the contrary, adaptation to the new conditions of life was difficult and complex but, once accomplished, it formed the

basis upon which the reptiles and all the classes deriving from them developed.

THE REPTILE: AN IMPORTANT EVOLUTIONARY MATRIX

Actually, in special circumstances that we shall see later on, the two classes of vertebrates that rule our world today — birds and mammals — derived from reptiles. This historical fact is usually overlooked: in a flying dove, or a running horse, we cannot see the reptile that generated them, and we tend to refuse the facts of the evolutionary process and insist on the independence of the three classes. But with a study of the long history of reptiles, we can carry out an accurate analysis of the phenomenon of "evolution" through its spectacular, great changes, which are usually called the processes of "macroevolution." The

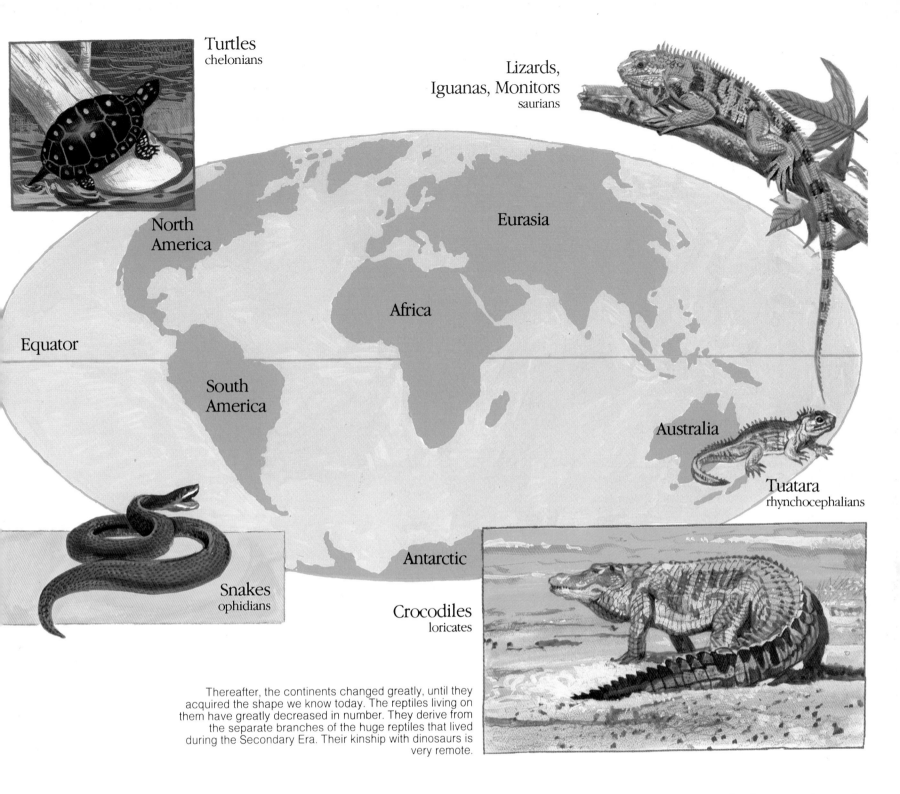

Turtles
chelonians

Lizards, Iguanas, Monitors
saurians

North America

Eurasia

Africa

Equator

South America

Australia

Tuatara
rhynchocephalians

Antarctic

Snakes
ophidians

Crocodiles
loricates

Thereafter, the continents changed greatly, until they acquired the shape we know today. The reptiles living on them have greatly decreased in number. They derive from the separate branches of the huge reptiles that lived during the Secondary Era. Their kinship with dinosaurs is very remote.

history of the horse, or better, of the horse's foot, is a typical case. It changed from three or four digits touching the ground into one single, strong hoof, suitable for running. But this event, important as it may be in understanding the evolutionary process, is trivial in comparison to the great and varied changes that occurred in reptile history as far as specific processes of adaptation. In short, the best class through which we can study the process of evolution and its laws, along with its spectacular flexibility, is the class of the reptiles.

THE GREAT DOMINION

Reptiles deserve all the respect that is due to a fallen noble. The reptiles are the remains of a great dominion that these vertebrates established on Earth, and maintained for a long time, tackling and overcoming the competition of new emerging classes.

The first reptiles appeared in the late Carboniferous Period, about 300 million years ago; asserted themselves with a first phase of evolution in the Permian Period, 280 million years ago; and flourished in thousands of different species during the whole Secondary Era, from 225 to 65 million years ago. They adapted themselves to running, swimming, flying, and to a herbivorous or carnivorous diet; they were either as tiny as pigeons, or as huge as grass-eating dinosaurs. During the whole Secondary Era, every corner of our Earth was firmly held by some reptile or other.

EXTINCTION

What is more, the reptile was the protagonist of an event that has perhaps received a little too much publicity in the popular press, and still strikes us today on account of the spectacularity and mystery surrounding it: 65 million years ago, the great majority of reptiles dominating the Secondary Era mysteriously disappeared. Much has been written in the past, and much will be written in the future, on the reptile hecatomb, because we still do not know what really happened.

A SERIOUS MISTAKE

Until recently, reptiles were used as models to explain the features of species that lived in the Secondary Era: today, this glaring error has at last been corrected, and it is acknowledged that ancient reptiles had a more complex and advanced anatomical and functional structure, from an evolutionary standpoint. More particularly, dinosaurs are being carefully studied today and surprising facts are being revealed. They will be explained in detail in the volume of this series *Dinosaurs and Birds*. In other words, the reptiles' sinister aura and the tendency to ignore or disregard them are not justifiable; these vertebrates have played an important role in our history and deserve proper attention.

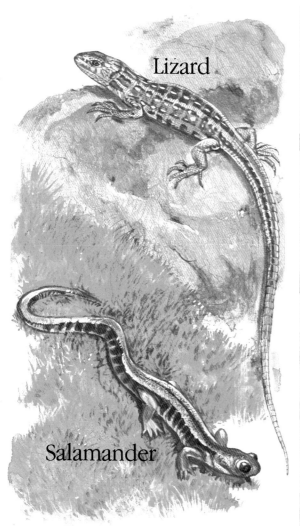

Lizard

Salamander

Lizards, which are reptiles, and salamanders, which are amphibians, have a similar shape. Nevertheless, there is a great difference in the internal anatomy and in the functions of the two classes to which they belong.

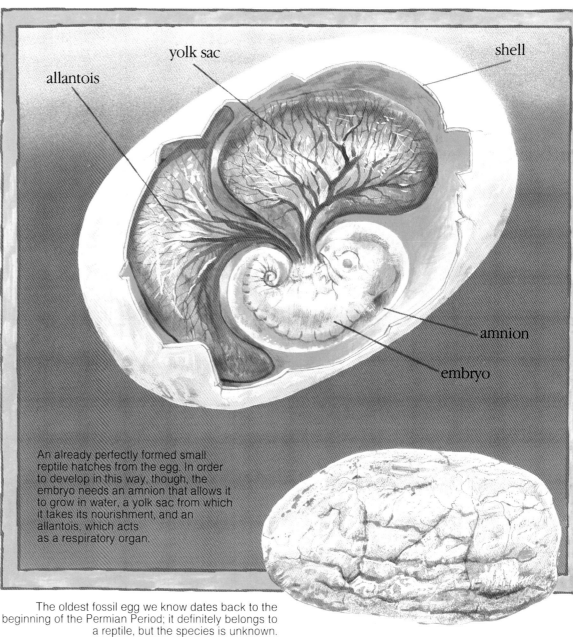

allantois

yolk sac

shell

amnion

embryo

An already perfectly formed small reptile hatches from the egg. In order to develop in this way, though, the embryo needs an amnion that allows it to grow in water, a yolk sac from which it takes its nourishment, and an allantois, which acts as a respiratory organ.

The oldest fossil egg we know dates back to the beginning of the Permian Period; it definitely belongs to a reptile, but the species is unknown.

2. WHAT MAKES A REPTILE: THE EMBRYO AND THE SKIN

AN ENVIRONMENTAL DIFFERENCE

When we observe a salamander (which is amphibious), and a lizard (a reptile), we feel we can easily see how reptiles derived from amphibians. The two animals have the same shape and the same gait, although the lizard is sharper and faster. Both hunt small insects. Only the habitats of these two animals are different: salamanders live in damp grass and ditches; while lizards live in rocky, sunny places. This last observation, which does not seem to be very important at the start, is the real basis of the profound differences between the structure of their organs, their apparatus, and the very functions of these two vertebrates.

A DIFFICULT PASSAGE

As we have seen in the volume on amphibians, it was relatively easy for an amphibian to derive from a rhipidistian; that strange air-breathing fish of the Devonian Period already had the anatomical bases for becoming an amphibian. Unfortunately, things look different when we come to the transition from amphibian to reptile. Amphibians lack the elements that can give origin to a vertebrate which is able to live — from its birth to its death — far from water. Either a new structure was created, or the structure of the amphibian underwent radical change.

THE PROBLEM: REPRODUCING OUT OF WATER

To reproduce, fish and amphibians spawn in water, and their entire development, from embryo to adult, takes place in water. The cells that form the embryo are all alive — even the most superficial ones — because they must continuously divide, grow, and form all the different parts of the animal's body. During the first stages of life, these cells draw oxygen directly from the water, to fulfil their needs. But an animal that wants to get free from the need to live near water must devise an expedient that allows its embryo to develop in water, but also out of it. This might

sound like a contradiction, an insoluble problem, but the reptiles, for the first time in the history of evolution, managed to solve it.

THE SOLUTION: A NEW EGG

The reptiles were the first vertebrates to spawn on dry land, in nests carefully prepared, and sometimes even guarded, by the parents. The eggs, similar to birds' eggs, have a hard, yet porous, calcareous shell, which protects the embryo, and at the same time allows it to breathe. The great innovation is inside the egg. Very soon, the embryo is enveloped in a membrane, the *amnion*, which fills up with water and artificially reproduces the watery environment necessary for the embryo to develop. Thus, the embryo is "in" the water, but the egg is laid "out of" the water; the problem is solved, the contradiction overcome. And inside the reptile's eggs is the *yolk sac*, containing highly nutritious substances necessary for the embryo's growth; then, there is the *allantois*, used as a respiratory organ, and for collecting the waste matter from the embryo's kidneys. With the aid of these three new devices — they will be taken up by birds and mammals as well — the embryo proceeds with its development. When it is perfectly formed, it hatches, and begins an independent adult life.

horny surface layer
that will be shed

detachment line

living cell layer that
will undergo hornification
after sloughing

layer of cells
that forms new layers
by splitting

Above: section of the skin of a sloughing reptile
under the microscope (snake, lizard).
Below: section of the skin of a reptile that does not
slough (crocodile, turtle).

horny surface layer
that is never shed

middle layer

Malpighian layer,
where cells split
and produce new
horny substance

loose derm layer,
where the bony
plates are, as in turtles

Grass snake

A specimen of Natrix natrix, the grass snake, during its sloughing. To aid in this
process, snakes rub themselves against the ground.

THE USES OF REPTILE SKIN

Many commonly used, high-quality, expensive objects are made out of reptile skin. For instance, large numbers of crocodiles have to be bred and then killed while still young to obtain skins with small scales.

THE PROBLEM: SAVING WATER

Amphibians dry up and soon die when taken from their natural environment and exposed to the air. Their skin consists of living, "bare" cells, which let the water contained in their body evaporate. Adult reptiles must also tackle this problem, and find the best way of saving every single molecule of that essential liquid which, from the inside out, allows their bodies to live.

THE SOLUTION: A NEW SKIN

The composition of the different layers of the reptile's skin is very complex; the following is a simplified explanation. There is a deep layer made of living cells that keep on dividing and creating new cells. These slowly move toward the surface and, as they grow old, they produce a new molecule, *keratin*, the same substance our fingernails are made of. When a cell dies, only a thin sheet of keratin is left. These small sheets, flattened and closely linked to one another, form the outside layer of the reptile's skin, the so-called hard and waterproof *stratum corneum* (horny layer), which stops any exchange of water between the outside environment and the cells below. When it is very thick, the horny layer not only prevents water

from evaporating, but also provides protection against the violence of the outside environment. This is the origin of the large scales of crocodiles and the thin ones of snakes — the skins we make shoes, belts, and handbags out of — and the compact scales of the turtle and tortoise — whence combs and spectacle frames.

SLOUGHING

A body covered with horny substance can also be a source of problems. The body cannot grow, because the stratum corneum is by no means elastic, but extremely rigid. The problem is solved in two different ways. In crocodiles, and turtles and tortoises, the scales grow progressively larger, as new horny substance forms and accumulates on the edges. Thus, the body can grow as the scales grow. The way lizards and snakes solve the problem is more spectacular, and interesting, too. When their old horny shroud becomes too tight, they simply shake it off, just as we take off our clothes; but while we buy bigger clothes, they have to grow them. The phenomenon is called *sloughing* and we do not notice it very much in lizards, because their skin comes off in shreds; but the snake's skin comes off in one piece as the creature crawls out of it.

5

3. WHAT MAKES A REPTILE: THE KIDNEY AND THE LUNG

THE PROBLEM: SAVING WATER THROUGH THE KIDNEYS

An animal organism also loses water through an organ belonging to the urinary apparatus: the kidney. The transformation of the proteins that nourish a living being in the process called metabolism also produces wastes, *nitrogen* molecules, which must be eliminated, because they are harmful to the organism. The task is assigned to the kidneys, which produce urine, in which the nitrogenous molecules are dissolved. More particularly, in fish and larvae of amphibians, the waste containing nitrogenous molecules is *ammonia*. This very toxic compound is diluted with a large quantity of water in the kidneys, and then expelled. But an animal organism that lives far from the water, and needs to save water, cannot adopt this system.

THE SOLUTION IN ADULT AMPHIBIANS

An early solution to this problem had already been found by the adult amphibians, which had to face life on dry land: the waste product from their nitrogenous metabolism was no longer ammonia but *urea*, a much less toxic compound that can be eliminated with only a little water.

THE SOLUTION IN REPTILES

Reptiles, sometimes forced to live very far from water, have found a more radical solution: the waste from their nitrogenous metabolism is *uric acid*, even less toxic than urea, and it can be eliminated in the form of crystals mixed with feces.

THE KIDNEYS OF FISH AND AMPHIBIANS

As we have seen, there is a special organ in the urinary apparatus, the kidney, which eliminates the waste from nitrogenous metabolism. In fish and amphibians, it is called *mesonephron* and carries out its task perfectly well; but the mesonephron does waste a large quantity of water — all the water it does not need — because saving water is not a matter of life and death to these creatures.

THE KIDNEYS OF REPTILES

Reptiles, as we have seen, must produce a particularly concentrated, or even semisolid, urine (the nitrogenous metabolism wastes). Hence, at this point in the history of evolution, a new need emerged. In such cases, evolution prefers to take an organ that already exists and shape it to perform the new task. This time, though, there was something new and revolutionary. The old mesonephron of the fish and the amphibians, still found working in reptiles at the embryonal stage, was simply abolished in adult specimens, and a completely new kidney, the *metanephron*, took its place. Not only can the metanephron comply with all the tasks of its predecessor, but it can also save water by reabsorbing it from the urine, which then becomes very concentrated.

THE INTESTINE AND THE CLOACA

Water can be dispersed through the intestine, as well. The feces of fish and amphibians always contains a high percentage of this liquid, and its dispersion must be stopped. This time, there is a simple solution to the problem: the last part of the hindgut, which is very short in fish and amphibians, becomes longer in reptiles, and the feces that pass through it are gradually dehydrated. But this is not enough: in amphibians and reptiles, the intestine does not lead directly outside the body, but to a chamber called the *cloaca*, to which the ducts from the kidneys and gonoducts also lead. In the cloaca, the absorption of water both from feces and from urine goes on, so the end product is lacking in water, almost solid.

NITROGENOUS METABOLISM

Metabolism, or transformation, is a very complex process by which biochemical and energy transformations take place in living organisms. More specifically, the potential energy that is contained in food is chemically turned into energy that nourishes or maintains the very substance of all animal organisms. But this transformation also produces "wastes," chemical compounds that have to be eliminated. Thus, nitrogenous metabolism eliminates nitrogen, which is harmful to the animal organism. The organic molecules of proteins containing nitrogen, for instance, are "decomposed," that is, broken up, into carbon dioxide, water, and new molecules that also contain nitrogen, such as ammonia, urea, or uric acid. *Ammonia* is produced by many fish, and by amphibians before their metamorphosis; *urea* is produced by mammals, selachians, and amphibians after their metamorphosis; *uric acid* is the waste expelled by reptiles and birds.

Right: simplified scheme of the waste matter of vertebrates' kidneys.

THE LUNGS

The amphibian's lungs are two sacs with almost smooth walls, and they are not very efficient. So they must be assisted by the skin and the mucosa of the mouth. In reptiles, though, this is not possible, since the thick layer of horny substance that forms on the skin to prevent water from evaporating also stops any gas exchange. Thus, in the new class, the lungs must meet the requirements of breathing on their own. In such reptiles as snakes and lizards, we still find lungs like sacs, but they have rougher inner walls, divided into small chambers that increase the respiratory surface. In turtles and tortoises, and crocodiles, the lungs are more complex: they have a main bronchus, the *mesobronchus*, that crosses the whole organ, with outlets leading into wide breathing chambers.

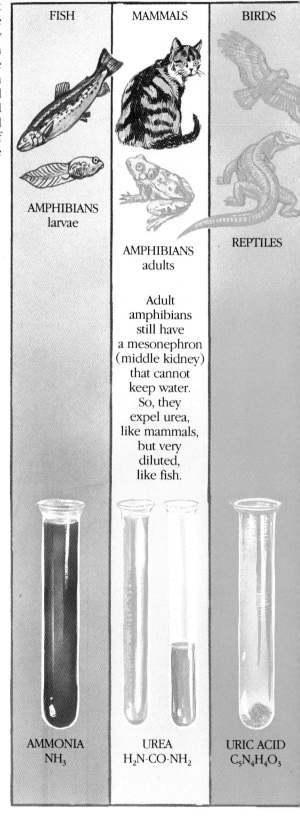

Opposite, top: the internal organs of a female reptile. Compared to those of amphibians, reptiles' lungs are much better developed and efficient, whereas the kidneys are totally new.

FISH

MAMMALS

BIRDS

AMPHIBIANS larvae

AMPHIBIANS adults

REPTILES

Adult amphibians still have a mesonephron (middle kidney) that cannot keep water. So, they expel urea, like mammals, but very diluted, like fish.

AMMONIA
NH_3

UREA
$H_2N-CO-NH_2$

URIC ACID
$C_5N_4H_4O_3$

Opposite, bottom: 1) Amphibians' lungs are shaped like sacs, with only a few folds in them and, therefore, with little respiratory surface. 2) In reptiles, the lungs have walls with many folds, and therefore, a very large respiratory surface. 3) In amphibians, the filtering units in the kidneys cannot retrieve water. 4) In reptiles, the filtering units in the kidneys have very long tubules in which water is reabsorbed.

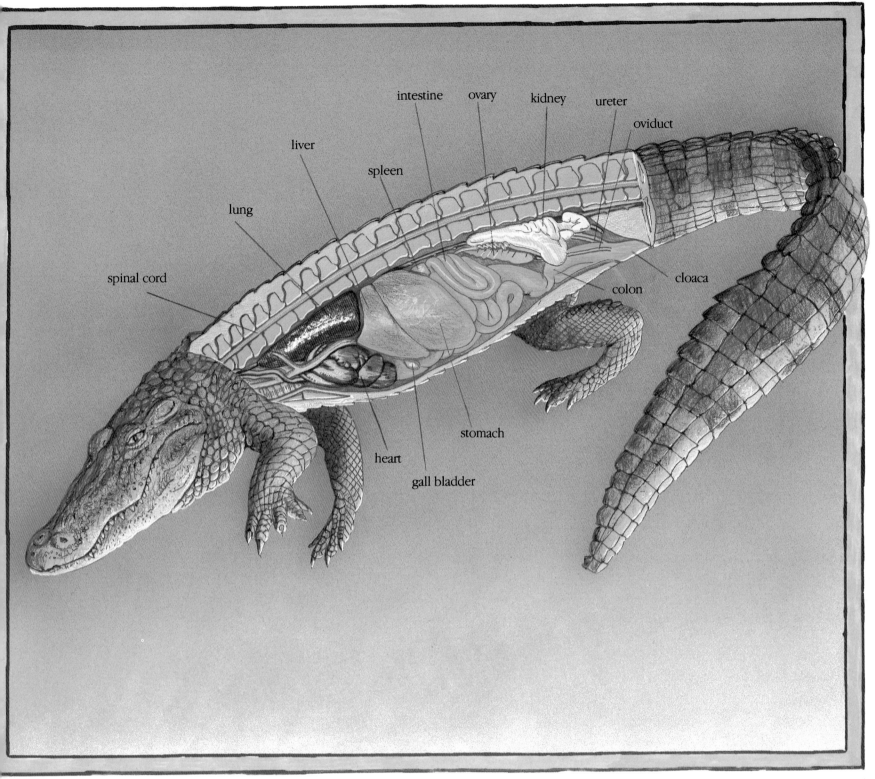

spinal cord
lung
liver
spleen
intestine
ovary
kidney
ureter
oviduct
cloaca
colon
stomach
heart
gall bladder

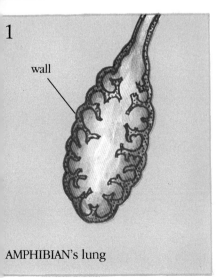

wall

AMPHIBIAN's lung

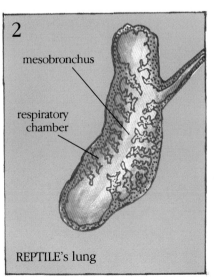

mesobronchus

respiratory
chamber

REPTILE's lung

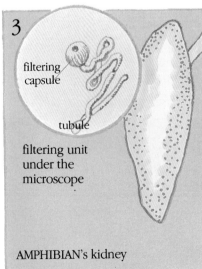

filtering
capsule

tubule

filtering unit
under the
microscope

AMPHIBIAN's kidney

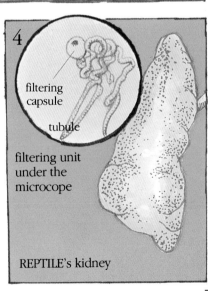

filtering
capsule

tubule

filtering unit
under the
microcope

REPTILE's kidney

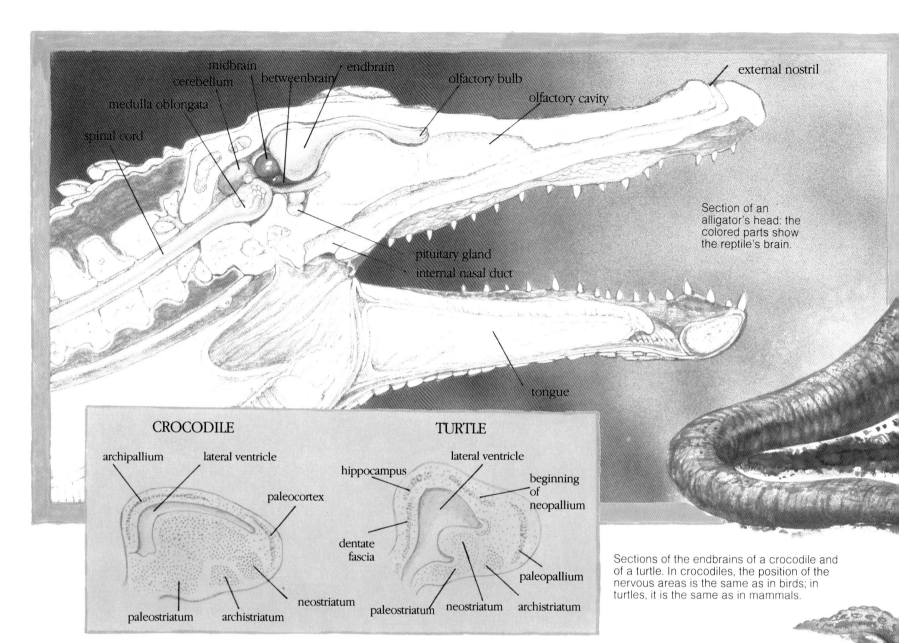

midbrain
cerebellum
betweenbrain
endbrain
medulla oblongata
olfactory bulb
olfactory cavity
external nostril
spinal cord

Section of an alligator's head: the colored parts show the reptile's brain.

pituitary gland
internal nasal duct

tongue

CROCODILE

archipallium
lateral ventricle
paleocortex

paleostriatum
archistriatum
neostriatum

TURTLE

hippocampus
lateral ventricle
beginning of neopallium

dentate fascia

paleostriatum
neostriatum
archistriatum
paleopallium

Sections of the endbrains of a crocodile and of a turtle. In crocodiles, the position of the nervous areas is the same as in birds; in turtles, it is the same as in mammals.

4. WHAT MAKES A REPTILE: THE BRAIN AND LOCOMOTION

THE BRAIN AND THE SENSE ORGANS

It is useful at this point to mention the main features of the brain of a reptile. It consists of various parts of more or less ancient origin that have different tasks. Starting from the back, there is the *medulla oblongata* (long marrow), which governs the general sensitivity and the movements of the head; then the *cerebellum* (small brain), concerned, among other things, with the maintenance of bodily balance; then the *mesencephalon* (midbrain), where the images coming from the retina of the eye are projected; then the *diencephalon* (betweenbrain), which governs all vegetative functions; and the *telencephalon* (endbrain), which receives olfactory information in the first vertebrates, whereas, in the transition from reptiles to mammals, it progressively takes over the general control of the animal's nervous activity, thus becoming its "real" brain. In the passage from amphibians to reptiles, the size of the brain increases, and another nervous area — which will become fundamental in mammals — gains more importance:

the *telencephalon pallium*. This is not the same in all reptiles; on the contrary, a strange phenomenon occurs that is difficult to explain: the crocodile's telencephalon is very similar to the bird's, whereas the turtles and tortoise's resembles the mammal's. Obviously, we do not want to claim that our class derives from the turtles, but the similarity might well be due to the extreme antiquity of both those reptiles and of man.

THE SKELETON

Living reptiles — much smaller than their huge ancestors of the Secondary Era — are larger than amphibians, so they have a more powerful and better ossified skeleton; but the basic features of the two classes are substantially similar. Only the number of sacral vertebrae on which the pelvis is articulated differs: amphibians have only one, reptiles have two. The skull, which requires a complex description, and helps us to classify reptiles, will be dealt with later on.

HOW THEY MOVE

The reptile's way of moving is substantially the same as that of the urodele amphibians, such as newts and salamanders (see the volume on amphibians in this series). Reptiles raise one leg at a time and move it forward, while the other three stay still on the ground. The sequence of the movement is also primitive: they move the right front leg, then the left hind leg; then the left front leg, and last, the right hind leg. This causes a marked twisting of the spine and a lateral swinging of the head, giving the animal the typical swaying motion of the snake. Reptiles have a truly primordial gait: it will take a long time before they discover the gallop or trot of mammals.

AN IMPORTANT INVENTION: ERECT STATURE

Some orders of reptiles of the Secondary Era took to standing up quite early on, and adopted an erect stature, walking only on their hind legs. Their

Diplodocus

Reptiles vary greatly in size: the smallest lizards weigh just a few grams (much less than an ounce), and measure just a few inches (only a few centimeters); the huge herbivorous dinosaurs that lived in the Secondary Era, such as the *Diplodocus*, weighed as much as 50 or 60 tons and reached lengths of 80 feet (25 meters).

Trachodon

Collared lizard

Erect stature was adopted very early on by some dinosaurs, such as the two-footed *Trachodon*. Today, after the extinction of the dinosaurs, only very few reptiles, such as the collared lizard, make short, fast rushes on their hind legs alone.

Below: the gait of a urodele, or caudate amphibian, such as the newt. Bottom: the gait of a reptile, such as the alligator.

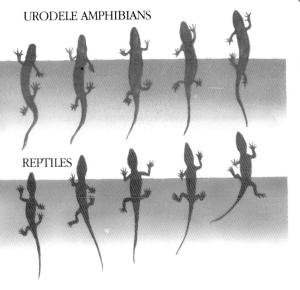

URODELE AMPHIBIANS

REPTILES

forelegs, no longer needed for locomotion, could be used for other tasks. The technique soon became very popular, and many species of dinosaurs adopted the erect stature, because of all its advantages, including faster running. But with the extinction of the dinosaurs, 65 million years ago, this new gait disappeared with them, and reptiles living today continue to move around on their four legs. Only a few saurian families can make short rushes on their hind legs, but they soon go back to their typical stance on all fours. Erect stature will later be invented all over again by a few orders of mammals, including our own, the primates.

DISTRIBUTION

During the Secondary Era, when the climate on most of the land above sea level was hot and dry, reptiles lived almost everywhere. Today, the climate is much more varied, and the distribution of reptiles has changed. These animals don't have thermoregulating mechanisms; that is, their body temperature is affected by the outside environment, and they usually have to live in hot or mild climates, in temperatures above 10-15 degrees centigrade (50-59 degrees Fahrenheit). That is why most reptile families live in tropical and subtropical areas, and the farther away we go from these zones, the fewer reptiles we find. The only reptiles living in Scandinavia, near the Arctic Polar Circle, are the common lizard and the viper, while there are absolutely no reptiles in Greenland, Iceland, or the outermost Antarctic.

The classification of stamps: 1) according to the theme (all animals); 2) according to the shape (all triangular); 3) according to the issuing country (all from Poland).

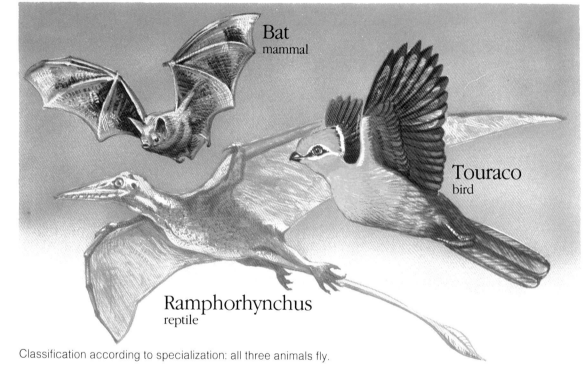

Bat
mammal

Touraco
bird

Ramphorhynchus
reptile

Classification according to specialization: all three animals fly.

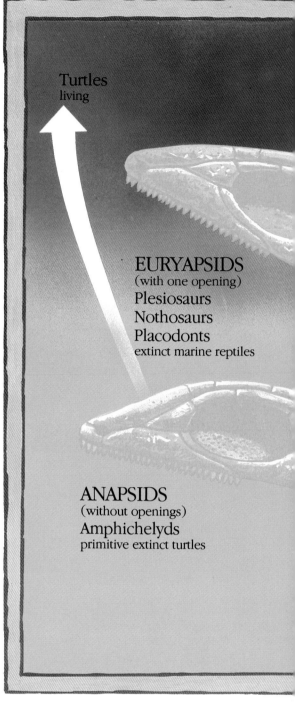

Turtles
living

EURYAPSIDS
(with one opening)
Plesiosaurs
Nothosaurs
Placodonts
extinct marine reptiles

ANAPSIDS
(without openings)
Amphichelyds
primitive extinct turtles

5. THE CLASSIFICATION OF REPTILES

HOW THEY ARE CLASSIFIED

Classifying living beings, animals and plants, according to logical criteria is a very important stage in any attempt to unravel the medley of different forms they have and functions they perform. There are various methods of classifying things. Some are based on features the things have in common. A stamp collector can either arrange his stamps according to their theme — animals, plants, astronautics — or according to the nation that issues them or according to their shape — triangular, square, rectangular. In philately, any such criteria are more or less valid, really; it all depends on personal preference.

With animals, things become much more complicated. We could decide to classify them according to their specialization, and put together all the ones that fly, for instance; or all the ones that swim; or the ones that crawl. But these criteria were already being criticized by the Greek philosopher Aristotle, who had found that dolphins do not have a fishlike nature, but a mammallike one, because their bodies are always warm, and they have mammary glands. Since then, a lot of time has gone by, and the relevant criteria have been defined much better. With the last century's discovery and description of hundreds of ancient reptiles, the problem arose of working out a method of classification that does not

simply take into account external similarities among the various animals, but their relationship and evolutionary history, as well.

SKULL OPENINGS

Many methods were suggested, but the one that won the most approval — and is still used today — takes into consideration the openings in the two side walls of the skull. They are called *temporal openings* and may or may not be present. When they are present, they are located in different positions in the skull bones. The actual purpose of the openings is not clear: maybe they are there to let the muscles pass through. All we

10

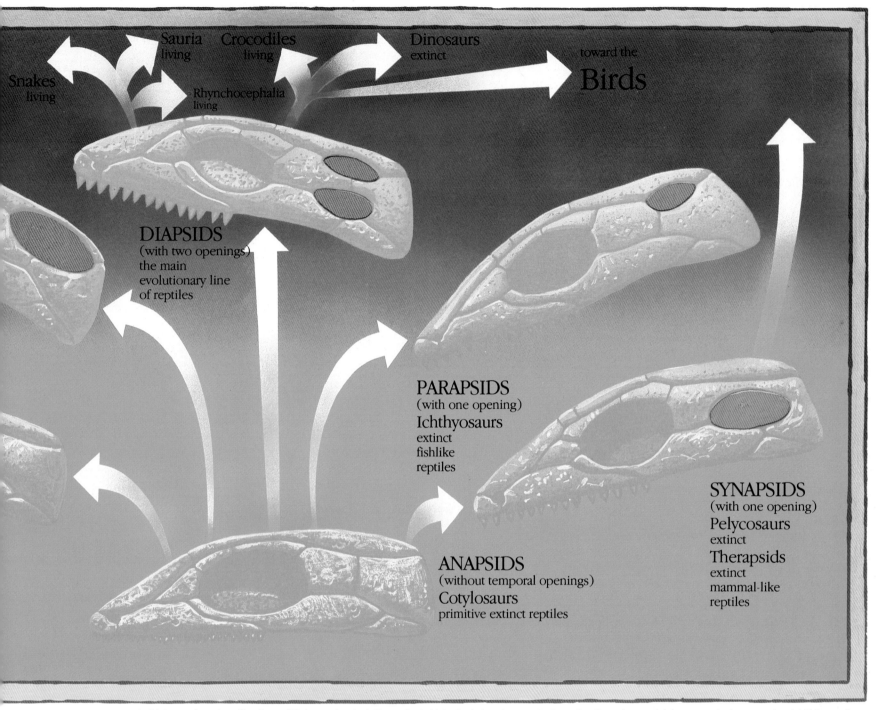

Snakes
living

Sauria
living

Crocodiles
living

Rhynchocephalia
living

Dinosaurs
extinct

toward the
Birds

DIAPSIDS
(with two openings)
the main
evolutionary line
of reptiles

PARAPSIDS
(with one opening)
Ichthyosaurs
extinct
fishlike
reptiles

ANAPSIDS
(without temporal openings)
Cotylosaurs
primitive extinct reptiles

SYNAPSIDS
(with one opening)
Pelycosaurs
extinct
Therapsids
extinct
mammal-like
reptiles

In biology, the classification of living animals follows their historical development along the lines from which a certain form evolved. With reptiles, these lines are established by the way the temporal openings (pink) formed on the side wall of the skull.

know for sure is that they have different features in the different evolutionary lines. The basic criterion for classifying all reptiles, living or extinct, derives from this observation (see also the two pages at the beginning and at the end of this volume).

THE ANAPSIDIS

The anapsids are the most primitive reptiles. Their skulls are made up of a continuous bony wall *without* temporal openings. Among the anapsids are the now-extinct cotylosaurs, the very first reptiles that appeared on the Earth, and the chelonians, which include both extinct and living turtles and tortoises.

THE PARAPSIDS

The parapsid group of reptiles have *a single* opening *almost at the top of the skull*. The group includes the

ichthyosaurs, very similar to dolphins, which were perfectly adapted to life in the sea. All the parapsids are extinct today.

THE EURYAPSIDS

The euryapsids have *a single* opening, larger and *lower* than the parapsids. These reptiles, too, adapted to life in the water, but they had exceptional shapes and dimensions. The plesiosaurs, for instance, looked like huge giraffes with long necks, and their limbs had turned into flippers. All the euryapsids are extinct.

THE SYNAPSIDS

The synapsids — a very important group of reptiles — have *a single* opening in an *even lower* position than that of the parapsids and euryapsids. In the therapsids — a branch of synapsids — the opening is very similar

to the mammal's. As we will see later on, our own class originated from them. All the synapsids are extinct.

THE DIAPSIDS

The diapsids have *two* openings on the side wall of the skull. They were the leading characters in the reptiles' great expansion during the Secondary Era, and they gave rise to two evolutionary lines that are still living today: snakes and saurians. But certain diapsids, the thecodont archosaurs, invented something new: with them, teeth, which used only to lie on the jawbones, became firmly embedded in special sockets that penetrated into the bone (Chapter 26). The new device proved to be very efficient. The thecodont archosaurs gave rise to the dinosaurs, which ruled over the whole Earth throughout the Secondary Era, with only birds for company. The only members of this group still living today are the crocodiles.

Coal comes from the fossilized plants of the Carboniferous Period, 345-280 million years ago. Their fossilized remains can be used to establish a record of how and when those ancient plants developed and died.

Toward the end of the Carboniferous Period, there were enormous luxuriant forests of horsetails and club mosses on the Earth. The amphibians, the first terrestrial vertebrates, lived in the undergrowth, in a humid, unchanging climate.
Here, among giant ferns, we see a large headed *Eryops*. On the edges of the great forests, there were drier areas with a variable climate (right), where amphibians could not survive, but conditions were ideal for the development of the first reptiles.

6. THE REPTILES APPEAR

CLIMATE AND FORESTS

The same as any other large group of animals, we wonder where the reptiles come from. The fossil succession is clear: before the first reptiles appeared, in the late Carboniferous Period, the Earth enjoyed a constantly warm, humid climate that favored the development of vast forests of trees totally different from the ones we see today. Club mosses and horsetails were over 100 feet (30 meters) tall, ferns were 30 or 50 feet (10 or 15 meters) tall. But the tallest plants were the Cordaitales, which could reach as high as 130 feet (40 meters). These huge trees grew very quickly, but collapsed with the arrival of the slightest hurricane, because of the weak structure of their trunks.

But as soon as these giants fell and disappeared forever, new specimens developed just as easily. The alternations created an undergrowth rich in decaying organic substances, seething with life. As it fossilized, this environment became the huge reserve of coal we still exploit to obtain the solar energy caught and held in store for us by the trees and plants of that period.

THE DOMINION OF THE AMPHIBIANS

The amphibians — the first vertebrates that renounced living in the water — developed, spread throughout almost all the Earth's forests in the Carboniferous Period, and soon conquered the undergrowth. The warm, damp climate favored their development. They were sometimes as long as 13 or 16 feet (4 or 5 meters).

The first reptiles appeared in this environment. They were the first vertebrates that were able to live out of the water, the first to overcome the great restrictions of the amphibians, which have to reproduce in water and cannot stray too far away from it. Now, which amphibians gave origin to the reptiles, and how did the sensational transition occur? This question is interesting because the event is one of the most important in the history of vertebrates.

Fossil of *Seymouria baylorensis* found in Texas, in the Permian Period layers. This animal had both amphibian and reptilian features, which has led certain scholars to accept it as the missing link between the two classes.

Seymouria

THE PROBLEM OF THE REPTILES' ORIGIN

In the volume on amphibians in this series, we examined one of their most probable ancestors, the *Seymouria*, which has the typical features of a fish, of an amphibian, and of a reptile. But the most recent studies tend to exclude it from the list of candidates. At most, we may consider it a member of an amphibian order which, with the complexity and variety of its features, may have given rise to the new vertebrate. So we have no reliable witness of this important transition in evolution; it is a serious gap in our evolutionary history, but there is still no reason to doubt that reptiles really did derive from amphibians. If we know only a little about the protagonist of this transition, we know even less about what engendered it. We do not know whether there was competition between the two vertebrates. The origins of the oldest reptiles we know of seem to indicate that the new

class appeared in the southern hemisphere, to the south of the continental mass called Gondwanaland.

HOW REPTILES DEVELOPED

According to current theories on the mechanisms of evolution, a new shape derives from one or more mutations that transform the features of the species in question. This is an over simplified statement, but we can accept it for the sake of clarity. Thus, we may assume that reptilian features occasionally occurred among the amphibians in the Carboniferous Period. But the animal that had the new features did not necessarily have any advantage over its brothers, who were "more" amphibian. Indeed, in the middle of the warm, damp forests of the Carboniferous Period, the new reptilian features placed the amphibian in a position of inferiority. If, however, the creature lived in an unstable climate on the edge of the forest, in

peripheral areas — and there must have been some — then those features made it superior to the others. Subsequently, the newly acquired features were repeated in later generations, and gradually became permanent features of the animal population; that is to say, they were selected once and for all. Hence, the areas on the edges of the great humid forests of the Carboniferous Period are likely to have been the places where the first reptiles appeared. There, the unstable climate, and the consequent possibility of periods of drought, made it necessary to develop features different from those of the amphibians. In these areas, there probably took place a ruthless selection of those organisms that were fitter for a prevalently terrestrial life, and it was this evolutionary trend that led to the development of reptiles.

7. FIRST REPTILES: COTYLOSAURS
(Anapsids)

Limnoscelis

Toward the end of the Carboniferous Period, around 300 million years ago, the first reptiles appeared on the Earth. Of course, we do not know whether their systems were like those of today's reptiles, because we only have the fossilized skeletons of those ancient animals. And the skeleton is often incomplete, although we can tell it belonged to a reptile from certain features of the skull and the spine. Maybe their system was not quite that of a real reptile yet; maybe they still had many amphibian features. But as we have already pointed out, the complexity of the problems to be solved before an amphibian could turn into a reptile suggests that the transition was not sudden, but gradual.

SIMILARITIES WITH THE AMPHIBIANS

The most ancient forms known today are classified in the order of the cotylosaurs, which had an anapsid skull, that is, without temporal openings (Chapter 5). They certainly lived together with many other orders of amphibians that dominated the Earth at that time. They looked vaguely like lizards, but were stockier and larger. The cotylosaur's skeleton is very similar to the seymouriamorph amphibian's; hence, it is logical to assume there is a relationship between the two classes. Indeed, the *Seymouria* was classified among the cotylosaurs, when it was still considered to be a reptile.

GENERAL FEATURES

An accurate description of the cotylosaur's skeleton would be very boring, but it is worthwhile outlining some typical features of these reptiles. Thus, we shall be able to recognize the different evolutionary lines, both extinct and living.

For instance, there is a small hole (the *interparietal foramen*) between the wall bones on the vault of the skull. It serves for the passage of the median eye — or *pineal eye* — which we will examine better later on, when we deal with the rhynchocephalians (Chapter 18), and the snakes (Chapter 24). This hole is a primitive element, already present in the amphibians.

The brain case, or first bony wall, is protected on the side, behind the eye socket, by a second, large continuous bony wall. This element is also primitive, and rather odd too, since the brain is thus enclosed in a double container. But this is probably not for the sake of protection.

The teeth are still very primitive in the cotylosaurs. The teeth simply touch the bone of the lower or the upper jaw, and are kept together by connective fibers. This is a very fragile form of dentition, so it is not surprising to find out that it changed a good deal later on.

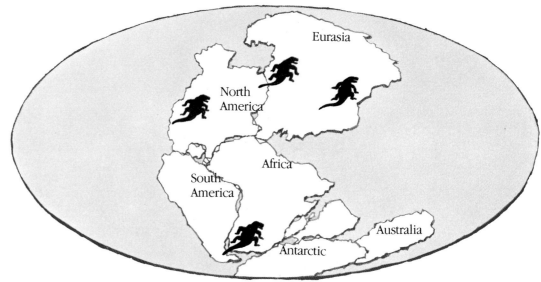

Cotylosaurs were distributed on much of the land above sea level, which formed a single supercontinent at that time.

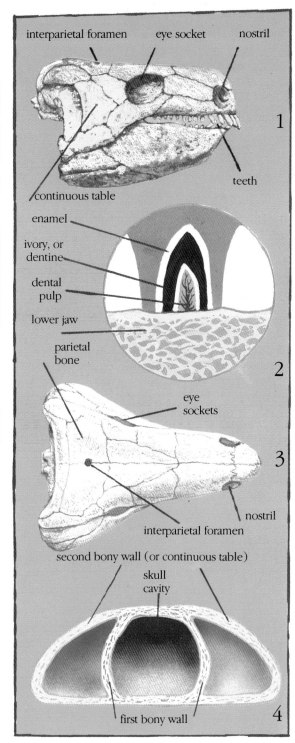

The first reptiles to appear on Earth were the cotylosaurs, which date back to the beginning of the Permian Period, around 280 million years ago. They still lived in wetlands. Among them were the *Limnoscelis,* a carnivorous predator found in the USA; and the herbivorous *Diadectes,* found in Texas: he had a massive body and short, powerful limbs.

Basic features of a cotylosaur's skull:
1) Side view from the outside of the skull.
The continuous bone table is shown in yellow.
2) Schematic picture of the tooth, not embedded in
the jawbone, but just lying on it.
3) View from above of the outside part of the skull:
note the interparietal foramen.
4) Cross section of the skull:
the cavity containing the brain
is protected by two bony walls.

THE DISTRIBUTION OF THE COTYLOSAURS

The cotylosaurs spread very quickly, one reason being that the Earth, in that period, was made up of a single supercontinent. Fossils of cotylosaurs have been found in Asia, Europe, North America, and South Africa; that is, in very disparate areas, which an animal that is only able to move on dry land, very slowly and sluggishly, would have had no chance whatever of reaching. But the cotylosaurs were present in all those places as early as the end of the Carboniferous Period.

SOME EXAMPLES

The best-known cotylosaur is the *Limnoscelis.* A whole skeleton was found in soil that must have been swampy during the Carboniferous Period when the animal died. Hence the hypothesis that the *Limnoscelis,* like the other cotylosaurs, still loved to live in damp habitats, with plenty of water; they had probably not yet overcome all the problems that prevented them from becoming totally free from the precious element. The *Limnoscelis,* a carnivore, was

no more than 5 feet (1.5 meters) long. Hence, it was much smaller than the giant amphibians that lived in the same period. Another reptile at that time was the *Diadectes,* a herbivore whose fossil remains have been found in Texas.

8. THE PERMIAN PERIOD: A NEW STAGE

ONE HABITAT FOR THE AMPHIBIANS, ANOTHER FOR THE REPTILES

During the last few million years of the Carboniferous Period, the Earth was still mostly covered with enormous forests inhabited both by the amphibians and by the first reptiles. But the two classes of vertebrates lived in different habitats. The amphibians prevailed in humid areas that had an abundance of water, whereas the reptiles preferred drier, though not arid, environments. It is difficult for us to imagine competition between the better developed amphibians and the first few reptiles, which could not make themselves felt as a new power yet. The first cotylosaurs were not very specialized — which is typical of intermediate forms — and were not able to compete with better developed animals.

CLIMATE AND PLANTS CHANGE: THE AMPHIBIANS BECOME EXTINCT

However, certain events changed this situation. The climate, which had been quite stable during the Carboniferous Period, for over 60 million years, started to become varied. The following period, the Permian, started with a sharp wave of intense cold that was perhaps the first glaciation on the Earth. Ice at the North and South Poles, and on the highest mountains, became thicker and removed large quantities of water from the other parts of the Earth. The seas became shallower, ponds and wetlands dried up, and the environment became more and more hostile for the amphibians, which either started to become extinct, one by one, or managed to survive in the few damp oases that still remained here and there. In the second part of the Permian Period, this cold, dry climate was followed by a hot, dry climate that engendered a deep change in the plant life. Ferns, horsetails, and all the vascular cryptogams that had made the Earth green for many millions of years survived only in the restricted tropical areas where we still find them today. In their place, the *gymnosperms* appeared and developed, and went on to dominate during the following Secondary Era. Some of them, such as the *Williamsonia* and the *Cycadoidea* — a small palm with a similar trunk to that of the pineapple tree, covered with flowers — are now extinct. Others, such as ginkgo, or maidenhair trees, monkey puzzles, cypresses, yews, sequoias, fir trees, cedars, larches, and pine trees, are still living. Since they were able to live and reproduce in a dry environment, these new trees set the stage for one of the most sensational events in the history of the vertebrates: the expansion of the reptiles.

THE ERA OF THE REPTILES BEGINS

The hot, dry climate that beset the Earth in the second half of the Permian Period, around 250 million years ago, remained incredibly stable until the end of the Cretaceous Period, almost 65 million years ago. The very long heat wave favored the development of the reptiles which, like the amphibians, are *poikilothermic*

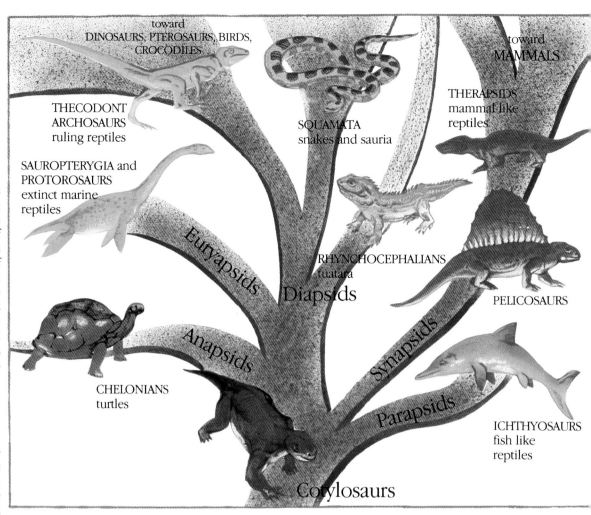

toward DINOSAURS, PTEROSAURS, BIRDS, CROCODILES

THECODONT ARCHOSAURS
ruling reptiles

SAUROPTERYGIA and PROTOROSAURS
extinct marine reptiles

SQUAMATA
snakes and sauria

toward MAMMALS

THERAPSIDS
mammal-like reptiles

RHYNCHOCEPHALIANS
tuatara

Eutyapsids

Diapsids

PELICOSAURS

Anapsids

Synapsids

Parapsids

CHELONIANS
turtles

ICHTHYOSAURS
fish-like reptiles

Cotylosaurs

The cotylosaurs, the oldest reptiles we know today, probably gave rise to the different evolutionary lines of reptiles.

(or cold-blooded); that is, they cannot keep a constant temperature in their bodies, and can bear neither intense cold nor intense heat. During the Permian Period, the new class of reptiles expanded and conquered every remote corner of the Earth, air and water included. The first vertebrates able to fly originated from the reptiles, while many evolutionary lines left the land to colonize the sea.

The cotylosaurs were the starting point of the different evolutionary lines of reptiles. The *Pareiasaurus*, for instance, moved about with a certain self-confidence in the new environment, with the snow far away, and abundant gymnosperms. It was a stocky animal, about 10 feet (3 meters) long, and it had an anapsid skull. It was not aggressive, but fed on grass and herbs. Its fossil remains date back to the early Permian Period, and have been found in South Africa and Russia. New forms originated from the cotylosaurs, which became extinct in the Triassic Period. They were more developed and better adapted to the new environment (see the diagram above).

Opposite: At the beginning of the Permian Period, the climate became unstable and an intense wave of frost began to attack the tops of the highest mountains. The dry cold destroyed the giant but fragile trees of the Carboniferous forests, while the gymnosperms made their first appearance. Some of these plants are extinct today (the *Cicadoydea*, which bore flowers, and the *Williamsonia*), and others live on, such as firs, larches, yews, pines, cypresses and sequoias. A cotylosaur, the *Pareiasaurus*, lived in this environment around 260 million years ago. Its fossil remains were found in South Africa. It was herbivorous, about 10 feet (3 meters) long, and had a massive body and huge limbs.

THE GYMNOSPERMS

This kind of plant, which had absolute dominion throughout the whole Secondary Era, is still well represented today, especially by the conifers. Both the extinct species and the living ones have tall wooden trunks; many are evergreens, and most live long lives. The plant's flowers, male and female, do not have a very wide range of colors, because fertilization mainly occurs by means of the pollen brought in by the wind. Their trunks are stronger and more resistant than the vascular cryptogams, and this enables the trees to grow in large forests with very little decaying organic substance in the undergrowth.

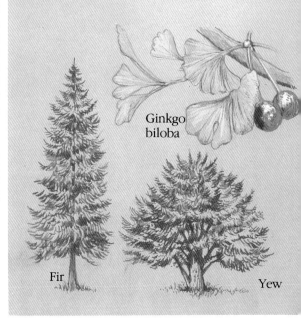

Ginkgo biloba

Fir

Yew

Pareiasaurus

Cycadoidea

Williamsonia

Dorsal (opposite) and ventral (opposite page) views of a box turtle, a land chelonian of North America. It owes its name to its ability to completely close the openings in its armor and stay well protected in its very convex shell.

Box turtle

Anapsid skull.

Triassochelys

In the Triassic Period, about 220 million years ago, there existed reptiles that already had all the features of the chelonians, such as the *Triassochelys* and the *Proganochelys* shown here.

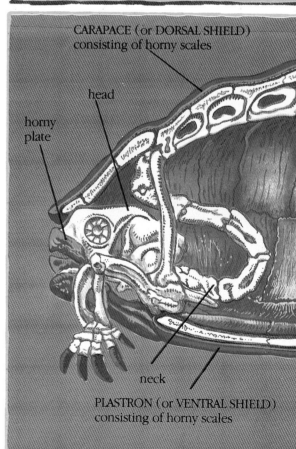

CARAPACE (or DORSAL SHIELD) consisting of horny scales

head

horny plate

neck

PLASTRON (or VENTRAL SHIELD) consisting of horny scales

9. TORTOISES AND TURTLES: GENERAL FEATURES
(Chelonian Anapsids)

AN ANIMAL THAT NEVER CHANGES

One of the most ancient groups of reptiles, along with the cotylosaurs, is the turtle and tortoise group. In ordinary usage, the generic term "tortoise" indicates the unmistakable group of armored reptiles classified in zoology in the order of *chelonians*, or *testudines*. The first specimens appeared during the Permian Period, around 250 million years ago, as is proven by a fossil from that era that has turtle features. During the following period, the Triassic, 200 million years ago, the skeleton of the chelonians had already developed a well-defined shape, and it has not changed much since then, which proves how very primitive and inflexible these creatures were, and still are. Today's turtles and tortoises are very similar to those of the Triassic Period. The same exceptional inability to develop is to be found only in sharks (see the volume of this series on *Marine Life*). All the other groups of

vertebrates were adaptable enough to proceed with their evolution.

THE CHELONIAN SKELETON

Like the cotylosaurs, these reptiles have an anapsid skull; that is, without temporal openings (Chapter 5). And they have one really exceptional feature: two powerful bony shields for protecting the body, which came about through the fusion of bones already present — vertebrae and ribs — with new bony parts.

The *carapace*, or upper shield, is formed by a central line of bony plates that developed from the vertebrae of the spine, with two series of plates that developed from the ribs at the sides. The upper shield is completed by a peripheral line of newly formed bony plates.

The *plastron*, or lower shield, is formed by bones from the pectoral girdle of the ribs, and by the abdominal ribs.

In the box turtle, as in any other turtle, the skeleton is an integral part of the armor; the animal cannot leave its "little house."

Proganochelys

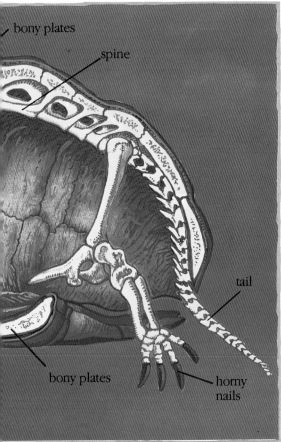

bony plates

spine

tail

bony plates

horny nails

The two shields are welded on the sides, but they have openings in the front and back to let the head, legs, and tail out. The hardness of these bony shields is further enhanced by large epidermal horny scales on the bony plates: they form the external part of the shell, the one we can see. In chelonians that have left the land to live in the sea, the bony shields are much lighter, but they have not disappeared completely.

When threatened, certain chelonians can pull their heads and limbs straight back into the shield. Many others cannot, because there is not enough room inside their shells; if they pull their heads in, they have to leave their limbs out, and vice versa. Also, the rather special conformation of their necks is important. The *pleurodire* (side-necked) turtles pull their heads in by bending the vertebrae of their necks to one side horizontally; the *cryptodire* (hidden-necked) turtles do the same thing by bending their vertebrae into a vertical curve.

LOCOMOTION

When they walk on land, chelonians have the same clumsy gait as the urodele amphibians: they have legs at their sides, and their bodies tend to crawl on the ground with a serpentine movement. Many chelonians, as early as the Triassic Period, adapted to life in the water, both in the sea and in rivers, so their limbs turned into flippers, and they learned to swim. Movement in the water was much more efficient and elegant and also quicker, considering the volume and the by-no-means hydrodynamic, or streamlined, shape of their bodies.

EXTINCT CHELONIANS

Among the forerunners of these armored reptiles was the *Eunotosaurus*, a small Permian reptile that had the beginnings of an upper shield deriving from the ribs, which had become large and flat. There was no plastron underneath, and the animal had the overall features of an amphibian. And it still had teeth, which subsequent forms of the Triassic Period had already lost. The *Triassochelys* and the *Proganochelys*, however — which belonged to the suborder *amphichelydia*, and lived in the Triassic Period — had all the skeletal features that we still find in today's chelonians.

Left: section of a cryptodire turtle, which is able to hide its head, legs, and tail inside its shell. The typical carapace of the turtle consists of two parts: an external one, the one we can see, which is actually nothing but hardened or better-hornified skin, modeled according to a pattern with large scales; and an internal one formed of bony plates, which makes up the real skeleton of the animal, and provides the necessary support for the scales. The plastron also consists of a horny surface layer and a bony inside layer (the animal's horny parts are shown in violet).

Eggs and young of the snapping turtle.

There are two carnivorous turtles that live in the fresh water of rivers and ponds in North and Central America. Both are armed with horny sheaths similar to the beaks of birds of prey, and they feed on fish. The way they get their food is different, though. The snapping turtle chases its prey, seizing it as soon as it reaches it. The alligator turtle, on the other hand, uses a more patient method (see inset below).

10. FRESHWATER AND TERRESTRIAL TURTLES AND TORTOISES

(Chelonian Anapsids)

We usually think of turtles and tortoises as meek, vegetarian animals, slothful in their movements. Indeed, this is the case with the "domestic" tortoises, which we may keep in our houses, but it is not necessarily true of all the species.

HUNTING TURTLES

Two turtles living in North and Central America have very telling names: the snapping turtle and the alligator turtle. These two species, which can measure almost three feet (1 meter), usually prefer to live in the fresh waters of rivers and lakes. The snapping turtle is definitely the more aggressive and dangerous one. Its name comes from its method of hunting: when it is in the water, it swims toward the fish it is hungry for with very slow, almost imperceptible movements. Then, it wriggles in for the attack, and seizes the prey with the bony sheath of its mouth. It holds on tightly until the helpless fish dies. This reptile is so ravenous, and so good at hunting, that it can cause serious damage to the fish in its habitat. As if that were not enough, the snapping turtle sometimes comes out of the water at night to hunt the earthbound animals it encounters, even the larger ones. The alligator turtle is a fisherman more than a hunter, and it prefers to lure its prey. On its tongue, there is a bright red, fleshy protuberance that looks like an earthworm. The turtle waves it around patiently, keeping its mouth wide open. If the fish falls for the trap, it is swallowed instantly. The horny sheath, which acts as a set of teeth for these two species, is curved and sharp like the beak of a bird of

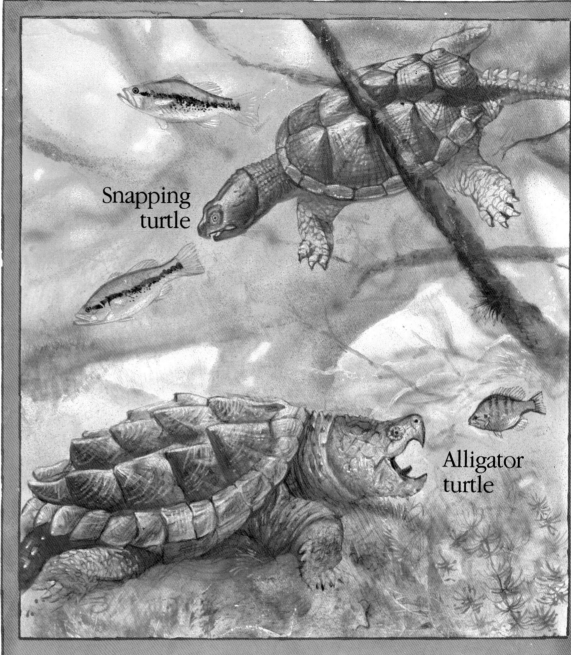

Snapping turtle

Alligator turtle

prey, and the creatures use it to tear strips of food off their victims. The food is swallowed whole, because turtles and tortoises have no teeth.

REPRODUCTION

The lifecycle of freshwater turtles is extremely simple: in the mating season and after mating (which takes place in the water) the female crawls out of her pond or river to look for a sandy place, where she digs a hole and lays between 10 and 20 eggs. Unlike marine turtles, freshwater turtles do not have many enemies, and the few eggs laid are quite enough to ensure the survival of the species. Once she has laid her eggs, the female simply forgets about them and goes on with her hunting. After a certain period of time — sometimes months, depending on the environmental temperature — perfectly developed little turtles hatch, and they too dash off into the water and begin their ravenous hunting.

TERRESTRIAL GIANTS

Galapagos tortoises, made famous by Darwin's studies, are the largest terrestrial tortoises. They can

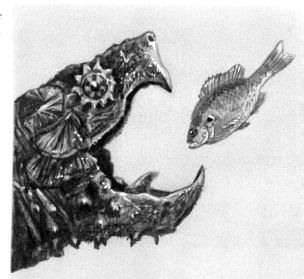

On the alligator turtle's tongue is a bright-red, fleshy protuberance that simulates bait and lures unwary little fish. When the fish swims into its wide-open mouth, the turtle snaps its jaws, and swallows it down.

Galapagos tortoise

Hermann's tortoise

Hermann's tortoises and Greek tortoises are very common in Europe and on the Mediterranean coasts. They live on dry soil and feed on leaves, fruit, and worms. They are bred as domestic animals and are kept as children's pets in gardens or even indoors.

Red-eared turtle

View of the front (top) and back (bottom) of the red-eared turtle, a small freshwater turtle with a typical doodlelike pattern. It is bred in aquariums.

The herbivorous Galapagos tortoises used to live in great numbers on the islands off the coast of Ecuador, South America, from which they take their name. They were almost exterminated by pirate ships and whalers that used to draw abundantly on this food supply when they sailed by.

THE SHEATH

We find the sheath, or beak, for the first time in the chelonians. It has the same function as teeth, and is made of a sheath of horny substance covering the upper and lower jaws. It is hard to decide which is more efficient, teeth or the sheath, but it is peculiar that not only primitive animals like turtles and tortoises have them, but also highly sophisticated, well-developed vertebrates like birds and some mammals.

be up to 40 inches (110 centimeters) long. Unfortunately, these gigantic animals are in danger of becoming extinct for various reasons: they were hunted for their tasty meat until a few score years ago; the wild, untouched environment where they live and reproduce is becoming smaller; man has recently introduced pigs and dogs, thus increasing the number of their natural predators.

PET TURTLES AND TORTOISES

In the Mediterranean basin and in North America, there live two species of tortoises that have always been very successful as pets. Hermann's tortoise and the Greek tortoise are terrestrial reptiles that can also live in our homes, because they are not afraid of man;

indeed, they actually get to know the person who feeds them. They are very tame and fairly intelligent. Their fame is due to the endurance of their body, for they can survive brutal crippling; to their longevity, for they can live to be more than a hundred years old; and to their ability to go without food, for they can live for over a year without eating.

The red-eared turtle, a cute little North American turtle, owes its Latin name, *Pseudemys scripta*, partly to an odd custom dating back to the last century: people used to send one another living specimens with greetings or love messages written on their backs. Nowadays, this custom has been abandoned, but the red-eared turtle is still kept in small domestic aacquariums, and is much appreciated for its gracious, lively movements.

11. MARINE TURTLES
(Chelonian Anapsids)

Terrestrial tortoises are not the only very ancient ones, though fossil specimens do date back to over 150 million years ago. Marine turtles have very old ancestors, as well.

AN EXTINCT GIANT

The fossil skeleton of a marine turtle measuring over 20 feet (6 meters) in length dates back to the Cretaceous Period. The *Archelon* — the name given to this giant species — lived in a period that was dominated by reptiles just as enormous, but belonging to other species. They populated dry land, air, and sea. It could be a coincidence, or maybe there was a reason we cannot grasp behind this general tendency toward giantism.

MARINE TURTLES TODAY

Living marine turtles are much smaller: the largest one, the leathery turtle, is about 6½ feet (2 meters) long. It is nevertheless quite a big turtle, at 1,300 pounds (600 kilograms), and is found in all the warm seas of the Earth, although its numbers are decreasing dangerously. The species is directly threatened by man, who hunts its eggs — which are said to be particularly tasty — although man does not eat its meat. Recently, it is facing a new danger. It has quite a varied diet and eats anything, animals and plants, and does not disdain even the stinging jellyfish. Hence, when it sees indestructible plastic bags floating on the water, it mistakes them for some tasty food, and innocently swallows them. The bags clog its stomach and the unfortunate creature, now unable to eat, starves to death a few months later.

THE DRAMA OF SPAWNING

The real Achilles heel of all marine turtles, large or small, is reproduction. During the mating season, large numbers of males and females migrate from the sea where they live to their reproduction sites on dry land. They mate on the way, when they are still in the water, and only the females crawl up onto deserted beaches — or beaches they think are deserted. The females silently make their way to the seashore at night. The weight of their bodies — no problem in the water — prevents them from moving freely, and their flipperlike limbs are much more suitable for swimming than for walking. However, the females do succeed in advancing onto the beaches, crawling awkwardly on the sand, up to places high above water. Here, each female digs a hole with her hind legs, where she usually lays a large number eggs — sometimes over a hundred — which she covers carefully. After finishing the job, the females find it easier to crawl back into their natural element, the sea. And this is where the troubles begin. It is very easy for egg hunters, especially man, to find the nests. All they have to do is follow the tracks on the sand. And even if the nests are not discovered, there are other dangers. When the eggs hatch, which they usually do all together, the little turtles dig their way through the sand to the surface and immediately scuttle off toward

the sea. On the way, however, they can become the victims of various predators, especially birds, which have learned the turtles' reproduction rites and throng the nesting areas in great numbers. The surviving turtles that succeed in reaching the water are not safe yet, because it is now the turn of diving birds and marine mammals to chase after them. The ensuing massacre is, however, counterbalanced by the great number of newborns, often over a thousand for each female in certain species. This is the only way marine turtles can survive. If we add man to all these natural fatal hazards, the danger of their becoming totally extinct is great.

EDIBLE MARINE TURTLES

Among turtles, the green turtle probably has the tastiest meat: it is the one used to cook the famous turtle soup, and combs and like objects can be obtained from its armor plating. Thus, the green turtle is much sought after and hunted. It is a large turtle: some specimens can be over 4½ feet (1.5 meters) long. It is exclusively herbivorous, and it may well be this diet that makes its meat so tasty. It is widespread in the mild, warm areas of all seas, including the Mediterranean, and in the Pacific, Atlantic, and Indian oceans.

The hawskbill turtle's habits and distribution are similar to the green turtle's. It too is in danger of

becoming extinct. In recent years, attempts have been made to bring the threat to an end by having the eggs collected and putting them in artificial incubators. When the time is ripe, the newborns are set free, and face no danger. This may be one solution to the problem, but it ought to be implemented on a large scale.

The loggerhead turtle may also be considered edible, although its meat is not as appreciated by gourmets.

All these turtles have one habit in common: when

The largest marine turtle that ever existed is the *Archelon iskchyros*, now extinct. It was 20 feet (6 meters) long and swam in the waters of the Cretaceous Period, over 100 million years ago. In that same period, some reptiles, the pterosaurs, had already learned how to fly.

they are not hungry, they come to the surface of the water and sleep blissfully, and fearlessly. It is not unusual to run into small groups floating while sleeping in the sun, and it is even possible to draw near and catch a couple before the others wake up and flee. But these animals are more often hunted while they are crawling up on the beaches to spawn. They simply cannot escape, and make an easy catch.

Opposite: marine turtles are excellent swimmers, because their legs have turned into flipperlike organs. However, they cannot stay under water very long and have to surface to breathe every now and then. The leathery turtle has smooth, thick, leatherlike skin.

Green turtle

Marine turtles, such as the green turtle, reproduce through eggs that the female lays in holes dug in the sand during the night.
The female immediately abandons the eggs and returns to the sea, leaving traces similar to the tracks of a tractor on the sand. The nests and their eggs, which are much appreciated by gourmets, are therefore very easy to find.

Hawksbill turtle

Loggerhead turtle

Leathery turtle

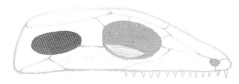
Synapsid skull

12. THE PELYCOSAURS
(Synapsids)

THE SYNAPSIDS

Synapsidian reptiles have a temporal opening in the lower part of the lateral wall of the skull (Chapter 5). As regards their evolutionary line, they derive from the ancient cotylosaurs that thrived in the second part of the Carboniferous Period, almost 300 million years ago. Their destiny was to be the protagonists of a great, important event, the development of a new class: mammals.

As always happens, their beginnings were slow, and there were only a few specimens. In the class of the synapsidian reptiles, there are two independent evolutionary lines, which are now classified as orders: the pelycosaurs and the therapsids (we will see the latter in Chapters 13 and 14). The pelycosaurs are divided in three suborders: sphenacodons, ophiacodons, and edaphosaurs.

THE FIRST PELYCOSAURS:
THE *VARANOPS* AND THE *OPHIACODON*

The most ancient and primitive form of pelycosaur known today was the *Varanops brevirostris*, a lizard 4½ feet (1.5 meters) long, which had no particular specializations. This reptile's dentition was not very differentiated, as in all the pioneer species, and there is evidence of quite varied eating habits. Very primitive features also characterized another pelycosaur living at the end of the Carboniferous Period, the *Ophiacodon*. This species has been studied a good deal, because it may have given origin to two totally different evolutionary lines: the ichthyosaurs, marine reptiles like dolphins; and the therapsids, from which, as we will see later on, the mammals developed. The importance of this species in the history of the vertebrates is clear; alas, not many specimens have been found to date, and it is hard, if not impossible, to relate them to the well-defined forms of ichthyosaurs and therapsids.

It was only in the early Permian Period that these two pelycosaurs asserted themselves as a dominating species. A good 70% of the reptiles then living on the Earth were more advanced pelycosaurs that were already highly specialized.

A CARNIVOROUS PELYCOSAUR:
THE *DIMETRODON*

The *Dimetrodon* is the best-known carnivorous pelycosaur. It still looked like a huge lizard, up to 10 feet (3 meters) long, with a very massive, voluminous skull, armed with powerful and sharp teeth. Its legs

Varanops

Ophiacodon

This plate shows reconstructions of certain pelycosaurs. They were stumpy and clumsy synapsidian reptiles that lived at different times between the Carboniferous and the Permian periods. The most ancient ones were predators: the *Varanops*, about 5 feet (1.5 meters) long; and the *Ophiacodon*, about 8 feet (2.5 meters) long. Their habitat was probably the luxuriant forests of the Carboniferous Period, favored by a warm, humid climate. The *Edaphosaurus*, with its high crest, was a herbivore, 10 feet (3 meters) long, whereas the *Dimetrodon*, which also had a crest, was carnivorous.

were still attached to the sides of its trunk, but they were thinner and nimbler, so it is logical to assume that the *Dimetrodon* could run rather fast. The most striking anatomical feature of this reptile, though, was the broad and thin crest running along its back, propped up by a line of bony rays. This odd characteristic was also common to herbivorous reptiles.

A HERBIVOROUS PELYCOSAUR:
THE *EDAPHOSAURUS*

This creature was larger than the *Dimetrodon*, usually over 10 feet (3 meters) long, but its skull was smaller and more elegant. The *Edaphosaurus* represents the group of herbivorous pelycosaurs living in the Carboniferous/Permian Period. This reptile had a broad crest on its back, too, which began just behind

the head and ended at the root of the tail. The high crest doubled the apparent size of the animal's body, which lead to a preliminary theory about the function of the strange appendage. The story begins with some of our living lizards.

THE FUNCTION OF THE DORSAL CREST

Some lacertilian species have folds in the skin of their heads or backs, propped up by bony bars, which the animals can stretch out in such a way that they look much larger and more massive than they really are. This theory about the function of the crest was initially applied to the pelycosaurs as well, but nowadays, on the basis of other considerations, it is believed that the task of the broad crest — which is always stretched out because the rays that propped it were fixed — is to catch the heat of the sun.

Edaphosaurus

Dimetrodon

eye socket

opening

skeleton of
Edaphosaurus

A *Dimetrodon*'s skull, with the temporal opening typical of the synapsidian reptiles.
We know it was a predator, because its mouth had many cone-shaped, very sharp teeth that differed from one another, just like a mammal's teeth.

bony strip supporting the crest

vertebra

THE FIRST THERMOREGULATION SYSTEM

The body temperature of all the vertebrates we have met up to now corresponds to the temperature of the environment they live in, and any variation, toward heat or cold, influences their organs as well. The pelycosaur's crest might well have been the first system invented by vertebrates to adjust the heat level of their bodies, though it was a very primitive way, and probably not very efficient either. Indeed, if the crest is exposed perpendicularly to the sun's rays, it absorbs heat and warms the blood flowing in the vessels; on the other hand, if it is exposed parallel to the sun's rays, the blood can get cooler. It is not much, but it was one step forward, providing a means of warming or cooling the body without depending exclusively on the outside temperature. The pelycosaur's crest was propped up by bony bars originating from the very long neural arch of the vertebrae.

Cynognathus

13.
THE THERAPSIDS
(Synapsids)

This order of synapsidian reptiles (Chapter 5) was discovered toward the middle of the last century, but it was only some time later that the experts realized how important they are in the history of vertebrates. Nowadays, many studies are carried out on these reptiles, especially on fossil records found in South Africa, and even older remains found in Russia. Therapsids developed the skeletal features typical of the mammals, so we may safely assume that our class found its origins in these reptiles.

HERBIVORES AND CARNIVORES

The therapsids appeared in the second half of the Permian Period, about 250 million years ago, at the

time of the dominion of the ancient, large-crested pelycosaurs. They enjoyed immediate success, and rapidly spread over the entire face of the Earth, which then still consisted of a single supercontinent. At the end of the Permian Period, 80% of the reptiles on the Earth were therapsids. Their anatomical organization was indeed more evolved. Their skeleton was in many ways lighter, more elegant, and suitable for running. In some species, the teeth became different from one another, specialized in ripping, cutting, or chopping. These new features made the animals far more efficient than the pelycosaurs, which became extinct one after the other. There were herbivorous and carnivorous groups among the therapsids.

The largest herbivores became as big as bulls. They were stocky, heavy animals such as the *Moschops*, the best-known species from South Africa, and the *Titanophoneus*, found in Russia. Their habitats must have been similar to our present-day semi-arid savannahs, where they grazed in large herds.

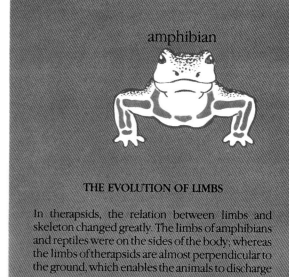

amphibian

THE EVOLUTION OF LIMBS

In therapsids, the relation between limbs and skeleton changed greatly. The limbs of amphibians and reptiles were on the sides of the body, whereas the limbs of therapsids are almost perpendicular to the ground, which enables the animals to discharge

Two large herbivorous therapsidian reptiles, *Moschops*, attacked by a group of *Cynognathus*, fearsome carnivorous therapsids, very similar to mammals. In the background, other herds of *Moschops* wander in the typical landscape of the Permian and Triassic periods, reminiscent of the savannah.

Moschops

Dicynodon

The *Dicynodon*, too, was a therapsid of the end of the Permian Period. It had many mammal-like features.

therapsidian reptile

mammal

their weight directly onto the ground, and move their limbs on an even level, just like the pendulum of a clock. So they could adopt new gaits, such as the gallop, at remarkable speeds. A perfectly vertical position of limbs was to be achieved only by the mammals.

Together with the herbivores, there lived the slenderer carnivores, with skeletons more suitable for running. One typical representative of the carnivores was the *Cynognathus*, about the size of a large dog, with an agile build that helped it as it chased its prey, which it seized in its long canine teeth. The most common therapsid living at the end of the Permian Period was the *Dycinodon*, a large, stocky, strange herbivore: its mouth was armed with powerful canines on the sides, while the tip of its maw ended with a classic sheath.

THE END OF THE THERAPSIDS

Their dominion did not last long: they were ousted, at the end of the Triassic Period, by a new group of reptiles, the thecodont archosaurs, from which the dinosaurs derived. In South Africa, the drama of this succession is quite clear: one large formation of the ground contains therapsid skeletons, and immediately above it is another layer containing only thecodont skeletons. Thus, the end came for the therapsids, too. But not for all of them, luckily.

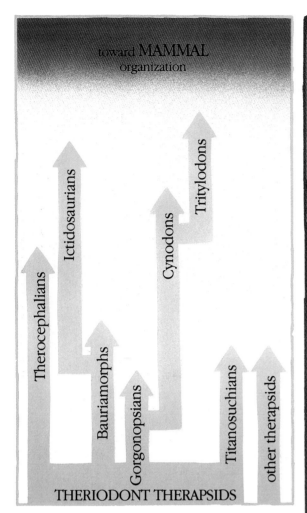

The arrows indicate the greater or smaller number of mammal-like features found in some theriodont therapsid families.

14. THERIODONT THERAPSIDS
(Synapsids)

MAMMAL-LIKE REPTILES

The *Theriodontia*, a suborder of the therapsids living in the Permian—Triassic periods (Chapter 13), are also called "mammal-like reptiles." The term well describes the strong tendency of these reptiles to acquire typical mammalian features, particularly as far as the skull is concerned. This is an important phenomenon, present in all theriodont families. The table (right) contains a comparison of the most significant features of reptiles and mammals. The graph (above) shows the greater or smaller quantity of mammal-like features in the various theriodont families. The longer the arrow, the nearer the family is to the mammals: the ictidosaurs and the tritilodonts, for instance, are so like mammals that it is hard to decide to which class they actually belong. There is no doubt that the first mammal originated from them.

WARM-BLOODED REPTILES?

One of the most interesting queries concerning the therapsids is whether or not they could regulate their body temperature, as today's mammals and birds do. Living reptiles do not have this ability, so it has always been assumed that ancient reptiles did not either.

There is no evidence of this ability on fossil skeletons, but we can check up on certain clues, just as we do when we read a cloak and dagger novel.

An animal that is thermoregulating continuously uses up a great deal of energy to produce heat, and this energy can be produced quickly with chewing, which accelerates the digestive process. The theriodonts were able to chew, because they not only had cone-shaped and pointed teeth for tearing food apart, but they also had specialized teeth for chopping food. Furthermore, they were endowed with a palate, which enabled them to chew and to breathe at the same time, just like today's mammals.

Moreover, traces of tactile-hair roots have been found on the heads of some specimens, which leads to the theory that such theriodonts as the *Anteosaurus*, for instance, were provided with fur to conserve body heat. And fossils of theriodonts have been found in areas that probably had a cold climate, and possibly even snowfalls. This backs up the theory that these animals were thermoregulating, because typical reptiles cannot stand temperatures lower than 10-12 degrees centigrade (50-54 Fahrenheit). That is why the startling idea that warm-blooded reptiles

Anteosaurus

Recently, reconstructions of theriodont therapsids from the end of the Permian Period have been made. They looked more like mammals than like reptiles.

REPTILES
missing
straight jaw
only vertical jaw movements
jaw consisting of many parts
cold-blooded: unable to vary blood temperature
without external ear
lateral eyes
teeth all alike
interparietal foramen
abdominal ribs
17 phalanges

Pristerognathus

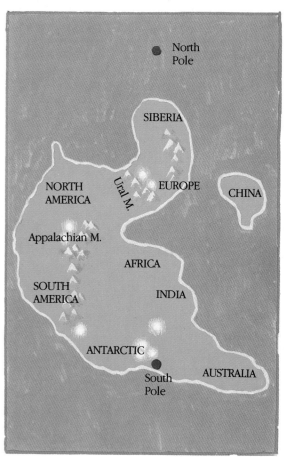

Schematic picture of the Earth during the Permian and Triassic periods. The main areas inhabited by theriodont therapsids, which probably preferred the cold, are shown in yellow.

	MAMMALS
	palate
	angle jaw
	horizontal and vertical jaw movements
	jaw consisting of a single piece
	warm-blooded: able to vary blood temperature
	with external ear
	frontal eyes
	teeth differing from each other
	missing
	missing
	14 phalanges

Comparison between reptiles and mammals on the basis of certain anatomical and skeletal features.

already existed in the Triassic Period is gaining more and more ground nowadays.

ARE THEY REPTILES OR MAMMALS?

The question now becomes quite pertinent. If we observe an ictidosaur's skull, we find many mammal-like features. Indeed, the only reptile feature in it is a small bone at the back, the quadrate. In mammals, this bone forms the incus, one of the three small bones of the middle ear. But if this animal had a mammal-like skull and teeth, if it was thermoregulating, if it was covered by fur, then why should we go on calling it a reptile? That tiny bone really is not important enough to justify our insisting on the traditional classification.

WHY ALL THIS HAPPENED

These almost, or maybe already, mammalian reptiles are at the center of heated disputes about the original reasons why the theriodonts tended toward their new kind of anatomical organization. One theory is that all the genetic information for a mammal was already present in the larger order of therapsids, and that it began to show through in a more or less observable manner only in the theriodonts. Another, more fascinating, theory makes reference to the dinosaurs. When the thecodont archosaurs — including the dinosaurs — came on the scene, the therapsids began to decline. Some of the theriodonts, in order not to be overwhelmed, sought shelter in the only ecological niche still available, the feeble twilight, or complete darkness. Since a typical reptile is unable to regulate its body temperature, it slows its activities down, or terminates them altogether at night. At that moment, any other animal can invade its habitat. So the acquisition of the main mammal features could well be explained in terms of the theriodont's adaptation to life in the dark. And our class, even the species that normally live in the sunlight, has all the typical features of nocturnal animals. In conclusion, the evolutionary line of reptiles with synapsid skulls (Chapter 5) came to an end with the theriodonts, but it may be more correct to say that the line went on with the theriodonts, which while adapting to nocturnal life, turned into a new class, the mammals; and the mammals evolved at a tremendous pace after the disappearance of the dinosaurs, about 65 million years ago.

Kronosaurus
sauropterygian euryapsid

Archelon
chelonian
anapsid

Metriorhyncus
loricate diapsid

Thylosaurus
squamate diapsid

Placodus
sauropterygian euryapsid

The plate shows various orders of reptiles that adapted to life in the sea or even in fresh water; not all of them, though, lived at the same time or in the same areas. The reconstruction is very improbable, but the main aim is to underline the marked tendency of the reptiles to move and develop in water environments too, competing directly with the older and no less specialized fish.

15. EXTINCT AQUATIC REPTILES: GENERAL FEATURES

This topic deserves far more attention than it gets. Popular images always concentrate on the development of terrestrial dinosaurs, sadly neglecting what had been going on in the seas. The fact is that from the Permian to the Cretaceous Period, this environment too was invaded by reptiles that were equally spectacular and impressive in their evolution. The reptiles were irresistibly attracted to the aquatic life; various forms, which appeared spontaneously in many evolutionary lines, modified their skeletal features to a greater or lesser extent, often following very precise rules, as they gradually made their way toward the water.

BODY SHAPE

Although ichthyosaurs (Chapter 16), which had fishlike bodies, are always mentioned as an example of how forms adapt to a new environment, marine reptiles came in many other, different forms.
The dorsoventrally flattened body protected by a shield of bony plates only came along with the turtles and tortoises (Chapter 9) and the placodonts (Chapter 17), an evolutionary line without any relationship whatever to turtles; so this kind of body must have been quite efficient. A body like a crocodile's appeared with the mesosaurs, which were

probably more slender and eel-shaped. Plesiosaurs (Chapter 17) were given a stumpy and heavy body, but this was compensated for by a long darting neck. So in finding a form suitable for the aquatic environment, evolution revealed all its inexhaustible imagination.

FLIPPERS

The new way of life also demanded a new way to move in liquids. The tail, the propelling organ of the fish, which is less important for terrestrial animals, assumed once more its decisive role in movement, as it had for ichthyosaurs, mesosaurs, and to a lesser extent, for sauropterygians (Chapter 17). Limbs changed very greatly in all aquatic reptiles, taking on the shape and function of flippers. The sea or freshwater species that did not completely give up the habit of walking or crawling on the ground still showed relative mobility in the different parts of the skeleton in the limbs; on the contrary, in the forms

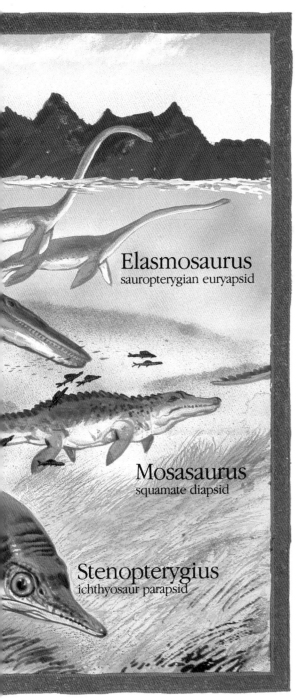

Elasmosaurus
sauropterygian euryapsid

Mosasaurus
squamate diapsid

Stenopterygius
ichthyosaur parapsid

Mesosaurus

The mesosaurs, crocodilelike aquatic reptiles, are not easy to classify, because they do not fit into the main evolutionary lines of reptiles.

South America

Africa

Atlantic Ocean

The green areas on the map indicate the zones where mesosaur fossils are found. Below: fossil skeleton of the *Mesosaurus tumidus*, which was 8 inches (20 centimeters) long,

that left the terrestrial environment forever, the bones and joints grew stiffer and the number of phalanges multiplied.

FEEDING

A common feature of all aquatic reptiles was their carnivorous diet, based on fish and other animals, which they caught in their very sharply toothed mouths. Only placodonts had grinding peglike teeth that could crack gastropods' shells.

REPRODUCTION

Reproduction was perhaps the most difficult stage of adaptation before complete liberation from the terrestrial environment. Some of the aquatic reptiles maintained their ability to move on the dry land— not for hunting, as their movements must have been as slow as today's sea turtles, but to lay eggs.

Ichthyosaurs and plesiosaurs instead remained

exclusively in the water: the egg developed in the mother's body and the offspring were dropped when fully developed. The exceptionally well-preserved fossil remains of a female ichthyosaur found at Holzmaden in Germany (see the two last pages) still contained embryo skeletons, while others were found nearby. Obviously, during her last agony, this mother managed to give birth to some of her young — but they too died shortly afterward.

FISH FACE CRISIS

The great development of sea reptiles, especially in the Jurassic Period, brought about difficulties for fish, which had been populating the waters of the Earth for millions of years; cartilaginous fish such as sharks, which ran the risk of extinction, particularly felt the pressure put on them by the reptiles. But fortunately for them — and for reasons we know little about — the marine reptiles began to squabble among

themselves. It is difficult to say who started it, but they began to eliminate one another, leaving plenty of room for the expansion of the sharks.

MESOSAURS

These reptiles also became fairly well adapted for the aquatic life, though perhaps not for the sea life. Mesosaur features do not allow us to classify them in the great subclasses we know; we often use the term *incertae saedis* for them, which means that we do not know where or with which species they can be classified. Mesosaurs did not enjoy great development; they appeared toward the end of the Carboniferous Period but were already extinct toward the end of the Permian Period. Their dimensions were small: they were no longer than 3 feet (1 meter), but their skulls, with enormous mouths bristling with teeth, made them frightful predators. In general, they looked like crocodiles, but the two animals are not related at all.

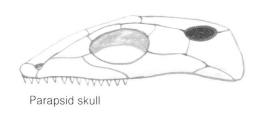

Parapsid skull

16.
ICHTHYOSAURS
(Parapsids)

CONVERGENCE

This is one of the most fascinating phenomena in evolution. The same environment and the same requirements lead to almost identical species. For example, 400 million years ago, cartilaginous fish (sharks) took on the shape of predatory fish, which we also find in ichthyosaurs of 130 million years ago, and in teleosts (tuna) and mammals (such as dolphins) of less than 50 million years ago. That is to say that starting from different matrices (cartilaginous or bony fish, reptile or mammal) the same hydrodynamic shape is achieved, with a strong tail to help with fast swimming. Thus, the environment makes its choices in one direction only, and the final result is the same.

Shark

Ichthyosaur

Tuna

Dolphin

ICHTHYOSAURS' FLIPPERS

Not only the bodies of these reptiles conformed to the marine environment; their limbs also changed very markedly, becoming flippers. Their legs became rigid, and the bones — such as the humerus and the thigh bone — became much shorter, while the widest part of the flipper spread out in a large number of phalanges. Indeed, a large number of phalanges is typical of a limb that has become a flipper, as we see from other reptiles that adapted to marine life, such as plesiosaurs (Chapter 17), and to a lesser extent, today's cetaceans (see the volume on mammals in this series). But there is a clear difference between a marine reptile and a cetacean. In reptiles, all the limbs have turned into flippers, while in cetaceans only the forelimbs have undergone this modification, because the hind limbs have disappeared, together with the whole pelvis.

Skeleton of the *Stenopterygius quadriscissus*, an ichthyosaur that lived in the Jurassic Period. The fossil, 180 million years old, was found in deposits at Holzmaden, West Germany.

The evolutionary line of parapsid reptiles — those with a temporal opening almost at the top of the skull (Chapter 5) — is particularly interesting because it includes only species that were perfectly adapted to sea life: the ichthyosaurs. These reptiles achieved such a level of specialization for the new way of life that they became very similar to dolphins or fish. Indeed, when we want to describe the phenomenon of convergence, it is impossible not to mention ichthyosaurs.

Unfortunately, we have no sure information on the stages of development these reptiles went through before they achieved their characteristic hydrodynamic shape.

THE MYSTERY OF THEIR ORIGINS

The first fossil skeletons of ichthyosaurs date back to the middle of the Triassic Period, about 200 million years ago, but their anatomy is perfectly well defined: slender body, strong tail with its fin, limbs that have turned into flippers. So we have no intermediate form to link these first reptiles, already adapted to marine life, to the terrestrial ones we know they derive from. The mystery becomes even deeper if we consider that ichthyosaurs are among the best-known fossil reptiles. We have many perfectly preserved, complete skeletons, and even a fragment of their skin has been

found. The marine environment, in fact, is particularly favorable for the fossilization of skeletons. Today, we know much more about species that lived in the water, especially in the seas, than about terrestrial creatures. Indeed, we have so little knowledge of the origins of ichthyosaurs that certain strange hypotheses have been put forward, such as the one that says they derived from pelycosaur reptiles of the *Ophiacodon* type (Chapter 12); and the one about their direct derivation from embolomeri amphibians (see the volume on amphibians) without going through the stage of cotylosaurs, considered the forerunners of all reptiles.

ALMOST FISH

Whatever happened, the first ichthyosaurs appeared in the Triassic Period, 225 million years ago, in the seas of the Northern Hemisphere, but they soon spread throughout all the oceans. They reached their climax between the Jurassic and the Cretaceous periods, 130 million years ago, when all the seas must have been swarming with shoals of ichthyosaurs hunting together, just as tuna do today. The ichthyosaur's shape, in fact, is very similar to that of a predator fish, and its teeth are typically those of a predator. Hence, we can logically deduce that their habits of life were also similar. For ichthyosaurs, like

all the reptiles dominating the Secondary Era, a slow but implacable decline started and culminated in their total extinction, about 65 million years ago, or maybe less. Their end is no less mysterious than their origins. They had reached an excellent level of specialization for marine life, so how and why did they disappear? And why did only they disappear, while other aquatic animals, such as sharks and bony fish, lived on in the same seas and thrived? We have no answers to these questions; even the catastrophic hypotheses about dinosaurs we will discuss later are by no means satisfactory.

Opposite: ichthyosaurs swam in the seas of the Triassic and Cretaceous periods 200 to 65 million years ago. These reptiles were so well adapted to marine life that they looked very much like dolphins, (the *Stenopterygius*), or like swordfish, (the *Eurhinosaurus*). They were about 6.5 feet (2 meters) long, carnivorous and viviparous.

Stenopterygius

Eurhinosaurus

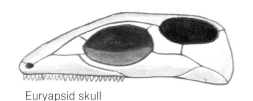

Euryapsid skull

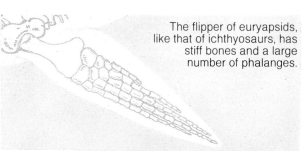

The flipper of euryapsids, like that of ichthyosaurs, has stiff bones and a large number of phalanges.

Tanystrophaeus

The *Tanystrophaeus*, which lived in the Permian and Triassic periods, was a protosaur, one of the most ancient euryapsids. In spite of its long neck, it was not more than 27 inches (70 centimeters) long.

Nothosaurus

The *Nothosaurus* of the Triassic Period was a sauropterygian euryapsid that could still leave the water and walk on dry land.

17. SAUROPTERYGIA
(Euryapsids)

The temporal opening in euryapsid skulled reptiles (Chapter 5) is almost on the top, and it is very big. The evolutionary line of these reptiles is extremely varied. It includes species that are very different in shape, dimensions, and habits.

PROTOSAURS

This order — which lived in the Permian and Triassic periods and is now extinct — is the most ancient of all the euryapsid orders. It derives directly from the cotylosaurs (Chapter 7). Protosaurs were small reptiles, similar to lizards, that led a partly aquatic life. The *Tanystrophaeus* was the most peculiar one: it had a very long neck, not because of the number of cervical vertebrae in it, but because of their length. Our parallel today is the giraffe.

SAUROPTERYGIANS

This order includes some now extinct euryapsid reptiles that lived in the Triassic and Jurassic periods, which generally comformed either to the amphibious or to the totally aquatic life. They are divided into three suborders: nothosaurs, plesiosaurs, and placodonts.

NOTHOSAURS

These sauropterygian reptiles — such as the *Nothosaurus* — were intermediate forms which, unlike the ichthyosaurs, reflected the change from terrestrial to marine life. They had amphibious habits, occasionally leaving the water for short walks on dry land, maybe to lay eggs and rear their offspring. Their legs were articulated, and could support the weight of the body. At the same time, they had some of the main features of typical marine reptiles, such as a long neck and a flat body.

PLESIOSAURS

These are the best known creatures in the sauropterygian order, partly owing to the abundance of fossils that have been found. They reached the climax of their evolution between the Jurassic and the Cretaceous periods, spreading throughout all the Earth's seas, and then gradually disappearing.

The main feature of plesiosaurs is a real source of embarrassment for experts in evolution. In the previous chapter, we have seen that the aquatic habitat leads to the development of a slender body and a slender head, along with a strong tail to provide forward thrust. The plesiosaur is the exception to this rule. Its body was not only bulky, but also stumpy and stubby underneath. Movement was not provided by the tail — usually small and not very muscular — but by four limbs that became large, sturdy flippers with countless phalanges, just like the ichthyosaurs. With bodies such as these, the plesiosaurs had no chance of becoming fast swimmers—quite the reverse. But the best weapon these reptiles possessed was their very long neck. It was often longer than the rest of the body, and ended in a small head armed with very sharp teeth. The technique they used for catching their prey probably consisted of a slow and cautious approach followed by a sudden flash of their long, darting neck. This evolutionary line of euryapsid

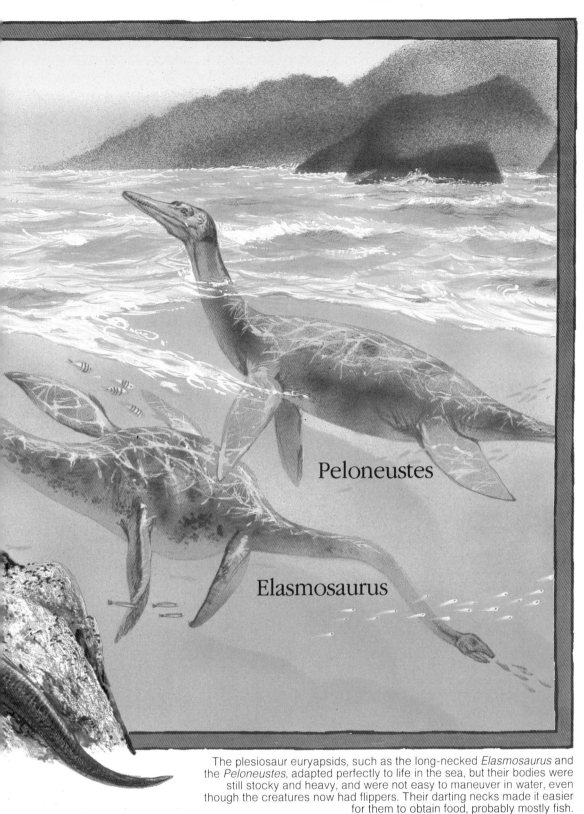

Peloneustes

Elasmosaurus

Placochelys
placodonta

Henodus

Placodus
gigas

The plesiosaur euryapsids, such as the long-necked *Elasmosaurus* and the *Peloneustes*, adapted perfectly to life in the sea, but their bodies were still stocky and heavy, and were not easy to maneuver in water, even though the creatures now had flippers. Their darting necks made it easier for them to obtain food, probably mostly fish.

The placodont euryapsids lived in the coastal seawaters during the Triassic Period. Many of them were armed with a strong carapace, similar to that of turtles.

reptiles had quite a successful existence, and as often happens to efficient forms such as this, gigantic species also appeared. The *Elasmosaurus* was over 40 feet (13 meters) long, while the *Peloneustes* measured 10 feet (3 meters) in length.

A HISTORICAL CURIOSITY

E. D. Cope, a famous American paleontologist of the last century, who was responsible for countless discoveries, made a big mistake when he reconstructed the first *Elasmosaurus* fossil in the laboratory: when he had almost finished the work, he had to decide where to put the head. The animal had two very similar extensions of the spine at both ends, but

which was the tail, and which the neck? After long reflection, he made the wrong decision, and stuck the head on the tail end, to the great delight of his colleagues, who had a good laugh when the mistake was revealed.

PLACODONTS

The last suborder of sauropterygians includes some really peculiar animals. Their diet, based on shellfish, changed their teeth into flat plates (which gave these reptiles their name) that could crack shells, while their lower jaw became strongly muscled.

Placodonts were marine reptiles, but their limbs — which had not fully turned into flippers — were still

able to shift their bodies on dry land as well. So they could lead an amphibious life. Some placodonts, such as the *Placochelys* and the *Henodus*, were protected by a dorsal armor composed of broad, bony plates, just like the turtle and tortoise. They spread throughout the seas around the coasts of Europe, especially during the Triassic Period, but had already disappeared when the Jurassic Period came along.

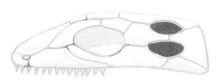

Diapsid skull

Classification of the diapsidian reptiles according to their orders and superorders. The derivations of each group are not shown.

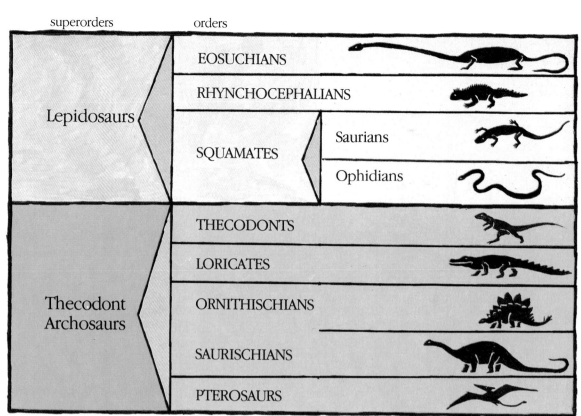

superorders	orders	
Lepidosaurs	EOSUCHIANS	
	RHYNCHOCEPHALIANS	
	SQUAMATES	Saurians
		Ophidians
Thecodont Archosaurs	THECODONTS	
	LORICATES	
	ORNITHISCHIANS	
	SAURISCHIANS	
	PTEROSAURS	

18. THE TUATARA

(Rhynchocephalian Diapsids)

The number of ancient and modern species, and the spectacularity of certain groups make the diapsid reptiles — creatures with two openings in the walls of their skulls (Chapter 5) — the most important evolutionary line of all. Dinosaurs and flying reptiles called pterosaurs were to derive from the diapsids. Moreover, all of today's reptiles — turtles and tortoises being the only exception — are diapsids. They are divided into *lepidosaurs* and *thecodont archosaurs*, two superorders with an important difference between them. The teeth of the *lepidosaurs* simply *lie* on the maxillary bone, as they do in all the other reptiles we have seen so far, starting with cotylosaurs (Chapter 7). The teeth of the *thecodont archosaurs*, for the first time in the history of reptile evolution, are *embedded* in sockets (Chapter 26).

Lepidosaurs are divided into three orders: eosuchians, rhynchocephalians, and squamates. For the classification of diapsids and the chapters in which they are discussed, see the table above, and more generally, the first and last two pages of this volume.

EOSUCHIANS

These are the most ancient lepidosaurs. The first species date back to the Permian Period, about 250 million years ago. But they were not very successful, for they were very probably already extinct toward the end of the Triassic Period. The *Askeptosaurus* of the Triassic Period (see the last two pages) looked like a crocodile, and measured about 7 feet (2 meters). It led a semiaquatic life, having a long tail for swimming, and short legs for walking — somewhat awkwardly — on dry land, where it laid eggs. It fed on fish and little reptiles. Another two forms derived from this primordial one: the rhynchocephalians and squamates.

RHYNCHOCEPHALIANS

While eosuchians were on their way toward extinction, the small order of rhynchocephalians was expanding. It reached the peak of its development in the Jurassic Period, when the Earth was ruled over by dinosaurs. But their evolutionary life was quite short; by the middle of the Cretaceous Period, they seem to have disappeared. From that period on, there are no fossil traces of them. Rhynchocephalians were sentenced to death more by the expansion of the saurians and ophidians, which had invaded the same

ecological niche and were faster and shrewder hunters, than by the formidable competition of the dinosaurs.

THE LIVING FOSSIL

It was once thought that the rhynchocephalians were totally extinct. But in 1840, a few experts were examining some lizards from New Zealand — which had previously been classified among the saurians merely on the basis of resemblance — when they came to the sensational discovery that rhynchocephalians still existed. Those living fossils were about 200 million years old. For all that time, their anatomy had remained unchanged, not to mention the fact that they had been living as neighbors of the dinosaurs! The news soon spread all around the world, arousing a great deal of interest among specialists. Expeditions were immediately organized to find out more about the creatures.

JUST IN TIME

But something bad was in store for the researchers. When white men settled in far New Zealand, they took

the cat and the pig with them. Reverting to their savage state, these did not take long to wipe out the rhynchocephalian population. Only one or two tiny islands, scattered around the bays of the two main islands, still offered hospitality to a few of those precious reptiles, which were soon placed under strict control in order to prevent their extinction. The first measure was the removal of cats and pigs, after which the reptiles were successfully bred in captivity.

THE TUATARA

The popular name the Maoris gave to our reptile was "tuatara," which means "sting bearer," owing to its dorsal crest of horny spines. Its scientific name is *Sphenodon punctatus*, a suborder of sphenodons. When closely examined for the first time, tuatara revealed just how primitive it was. Its vertebrae are similar to those of fish; it has no copulatory organs; and its metabolism is minimal, inferior to that of all other reptiles, and even many amphibians. Owing to this kind of metabolism, the tuatara moves extremely slowly and torpidly; it can also make do with just a few insects a day, because its energy needs are equally low. So it is no wonder that rhynchocephalians were

Sooty shearwater

Tuatara

The tuatara usually lives in dens dug in the ground and shares them with a bird. Here, a sooty shearwater is shown. It is not clear yet which of the two animals actually digs the hole and which is the tenant; though they are very different, the two species get along quite well, one reason being that the bird is active by day and the tuatara by night. The picture opposite shows a section of a den in the morning, the reptile going in, the bird going out.

The pig and the cat, brought by man to New Zealand, are the most fearful enemies of the lazy tuatara.

not able to compete with the more skilled snakes and lizards in hunting insects and small prey. They survived only on those remote New Zealand islands, where there was no competition.

The tuatara is nocturnal in its habits: it leaves its den only at night, even though it is not very hot. The temperature of its body is, in fact, exceptionally low, about 13 degrees centigrade (55 Fahrenheit), even when the animal is in the swing of activity (if we can call it that). In general, the body temperature of reptiles, even the toad, is higher—25 degrees centigrade (77 Fahrenheit)—which once again shows how primitive the tuatara is. But this reptile has at least one well-evolved organ: the median, or pineal, eye which specializes in perceiving infrared wavelengths; it works as a thermoreceptor, and informs the animal about the outside temperature. Today, the tuatara no longer lives in danger; it is the privileged guest of just a few islands where admittance is strictly forbidden.

THE SAURIANS: GENERAL FEATURES

(Squamate Diapsids, Saurians)

Saurians (or lacertilians) may well be the living reptiles with the most recent origins, as they date back to the Jurassic Period, about 150 million years ago, when turtles, tortoises, and crocodiles were already on the Earth.

ANATOMY

The saurians, lepidosaur diapsids belonging to the squamate order, have two temporal openings in the skull, but the lower one is not closed, owing to the lack of a bony part. Thus, the animal can open its mouth not only by lowering the mandible, but also by raising the upper jaw, with a movement that will become more evident in snakes. Its appearance is typically lacertilian, more or less stumpy or slender. There are also limbless species, similar to snakes. Snakes are still considered saurians because of the hardly visible depression of the tympanic membrane of their ears. Saurians have these beginnings of an external ear, which will develop fully in mammals.

REPRODUCTION

Saurians reproduce by means of eggs which are usually left to fate; some species, such as the livebearing lizard, keep the eggs in their oviducts, where the embryos complete their development and leave their mother's body when fully mature. On the inner surface of the thighs of many saurians there are strange glands, called the *femoral pores*, which are particularly active during the mating season, secreting a thick, viscous liquid. The purpose of this liquid is still to be discovered: it may be a means of attracting the partner, or it might make copulation easier. We do know for sure that it is closely linked to the mating season. The saurian suborder, which includes a little more than half of all living reptiles, is divided into 6 infraorders, 22 families, and 300 species. A comprehensive description is the task of a treatise on zoology, so we shall present just a few of the more interesting examples.

DISTRIBUTION

Since saurians love a hot climate, they are mostly concentrated between the two tropics. As you go off toward the poles, their numbers rapidly decrease and then totally disappear when you get to the Arctic and Antarctic. Saurians live, eat, and reproduce at temperatures between 10 and 40 degrees centigrade (between 50 and 104 Fahrenheit); if the weather turns colder or warmer, the creatures take refuge in their dens — hibernating in winter and estivating in summer — and patiently wait for more acceptable temperatures.

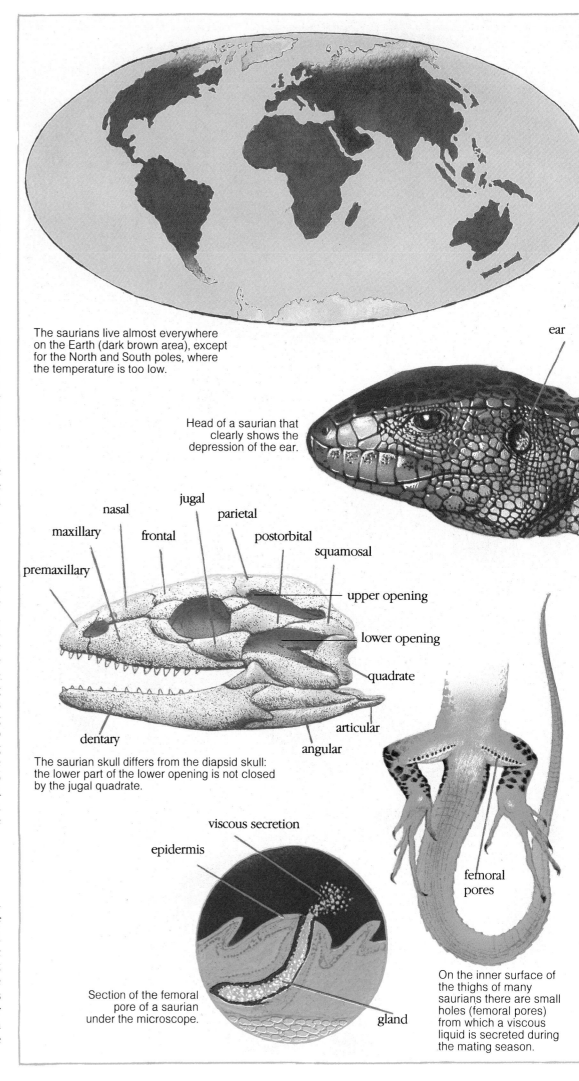

The saurians live almost everywhere on the Earth (dark brown area), except for the North and South poles, where the temperature is too low.

ear

Head of a saurian that clearly shows the depression of the ear.

nasal

jugal

maxillary

frontal

parietal

premaxillary

postorbital

squamosal

upper opening

lower opening

quadrate

articular

dentary

angular

The saurian skull differs from the diapsid skull: the lower part of the lower opening is not closed by the jugal quadrate.

viscous secretion

epidermis

femoral pores

Section of the femoral pore of a saurian under the microscope.

gland

On the inner surface of the thighs of many saurians there are small holes (femoral pores) from which a viscous liquid is secreted during the mating season.

Flying gecko

Diurnal gecko

Underside of a
Tokay's foot

Tokay

Banded gecko

Diplodactylus
conspicillatus

Leaf-tailed
gecko

THE GECKOS

Of all saurians, the gecko is one of the most ancient families, with vertebrae similar to those of fossil reptiles or fish. Geckos are cosmopolitan: they crop up everywhere in the warm and temperate regions of the Earth. They are the only saurians that can emit sounds. Indeed, their name derives from the "jeck-jeck" call they let out when frightened, but they can produce other gentler and softer sounds as well. All geckos have nocturnal habits; at dusk, they leave their dens and climb up walls and branches searching for insects. The gecko's eyes are very large and prominent, with thin, vertical, slotlike pupils; they have no eyelids, and have to run their wet tongues over their eyes frequently. Like all saurians, geckos shed their skins. Geckos are also very well known for their extraordinary skill in climbing straight up walls and other surfaces, even very smooth ones. The five fingers of their legs are flat and bear a tight row of plates; each plate is beset with numerous microscopic hooks, which find even the tiniest, most invisible hold on the wall. The gecko is very mild by nature, and does not fear man; indeed, it often lives on the walls of houses, and sometimes it even enters them when roving about at night, moving from one place to another in its continuous search for insects, which it captures and gobbles up in its enormous mouth. Geckos change the color of their skins a little: by night they are dark; in the daytime, they seem lighter.

THE LIMBLESS RELATIVE

In Australia live the *Pygopodida*, a member of the gecko family with no forelimbs and hind limbs that have turned into stumps. These peculiar geckos look like snakes, and they move and hunt just like them. The great length of their bodies is accounted for mostly by their tails, which are particularly slender and thin.

Artist's impression of a basilisk. In the Middle Ages, it was believed that if you looked it straight in the eye, you would die instantly.

The real basilisk (iguanid saurian) on the right, owes its name to the strange crest on its head that makes it look like a king.

Double-crested basilisk

Phrynocephalus mystaceus

Head of a *Phrynocephalus mystaceus* (agamid saurian) in the typical aggressive attitude it takes up to frighten its enemies.

The thorny devil (agamid saurian) is an inoffensive little animal that feeds on ants.

Thorny devil

20. IGUANAS AND AGAMIDS
(Squamate Diapsids, Saurians)

Two saurian families, the iguanids and the agamids, are very similar, but distributed differently. Iguanids live in the hot zones of the New World; while Africa, southern Eurasia, and Australia are populated by agamids. The members of the iguanid family range from reptiles just a few inches long, such as the Phrynosoma, to creatures about 5 feet (1.5 meters) in length, such as the Galapagos iguanas.

Among the iguanids, and the agamids as well, there are certain particularly agile species; to improve their running speed, they stand up and run on their hind legs. If this is exceptional in a living reptile, it is definitely nothing strange for the whole class; many extinct reptiles of the Secondary Era did, in fact, adopt an erect posture, as we shall see in Chapter 26.

MARINE IGUANAS

Until not so long ago, the rocky shores of the Galapagos Islands, in the Pacific Ocean off the shores

of Ecuador, were inhabited by large shoals of marine iguanas basking in the sun. That must have been a wonderful sight. Charles Darwin described it in 1835, when he visited the islands: hundreds and hundreds of iguanas, up to 5 feet (1.5 meters) long, lying in the sun, indifferent even to the presence of man, who could come right up to them quite confidently. In spite of their unendearing appearance and large dimensions — they are among the largest living saurians — these reptiles are totally inoffensive and quite meek. Their diet is based on tender seaweeds, which they nibble at on the seabed or on the surface. Iguanas are the only saurians that also venture into the

sea, but only in coastal waters, and only long enough to get food. But their numbers are decreasing irremediably, thanks to merciless hunting expeditions. Unfortunately for the iguana, his skin, duly tanned, is very valuable in the handbag and shoe trade. And it is so easy to capture these gentle, peaceful creatures.

TERRESTRIAL IGUANAS

In the same Galapagos Islands, Darwin saw and described another large species of iguana, one that had typically terrestrial habits. There were once large populations of these iguanas, too. Darwin relates the

Galapagos iguanas (iguanid saurians) at rest on rocks on the seashore.

Marine iguanas

Flying dragon

The "wings" of the flying dragons (agamid saurians) are colorful membranes stretched between long, thin ribs.

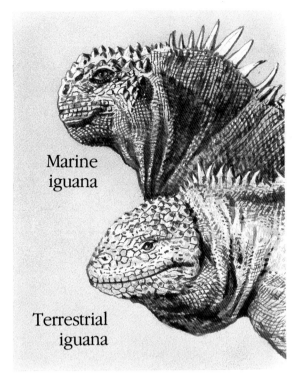

Marine iguana

Terrestrial iguana

Two iguana heads.

joining together various parts of the most ill-assorted animals. Today, nobody believes in the terrible basilisk any longer, but its name has been given to an American iguanid, which does in fact look like a little king, thanks to the crest on its head and back. The *Basiliscus*, which lives in the region stretching from southern Mexico to Ecuador, is no more than 30 inches or so (80 centimeters) long, but it is very agile and fast; it can even run on water for short distances, skipping along like the flat pebbles we all like to pitch over smooth water.

DEFENCE BY BLUFF

The *Phrynocephalus mystaceus*, or bearded toad, is famous for the way it defends itself. When threatened by another animal, it lies flat and motionless on the ground. If the danger persists, it rises on its legs and opens its mouth wide, making it seem much larger than it really is, thanks to the two stretchable, and very colorful, folds of skin on both cheeks. If the danger continues, the creature shoots outward in a desperate attack and tries to bite its enemy.

THE THORNY DEVIL

In Australia, there lives the strangest and ugliest of all the saurians, the thorny devil. Besides having a stumpy and ungraceful little body, this agamid — no more than about 8 inches (20 centimeters) long — is covered with tubercles, similar to stings, which make it even more horrible-looking. This explains why the scientific name for the poor creature is *horridus*.

THE FLYING DRAGON

This agamid also deserves mention. Along its sides it has two skin "wings" supported by very elongated ribs that can be folded fanwise. When they are spread, they bear the animal as it leaps from branch to branch. During this kind of gliding jump, the flying dragon snaps up insects in midair.

difficulties he had in pitching his expedition's tents because the ground was scattered with iguana dens. Unfortunately, today these large saurians too are running the risk of becoming extinct: not only is their skin highly prized, but their meat is said to be excellent. This is not surprising, because terrestrial iguanas feed on fruit and berries, which they gather when it is not too hot, in the morning or at dusk. When the day becomes too hot to bear, they rest, gratefully taking naps in the shade of bushes and trees. The terrestrial saurians are just as peaceful as their marine cousins, and they are not afraid of man, either. In the distant past, they had no natural enemies; today, even

wild dogs are helping to destroy this magnificent species.

BASILISKS

In ancient Greece, the term basilisk — which means "little king" — was already being used to indicate a mythical animal, endowed with mysterious, evil powers. The belief was passed on to ancient Rome and to the Middle Ages; indeed, the legend of the prodigious animal, which nobody had ever seen, persisted until the 18th century. For many centuries, cunning swindlers had created false basilisks by

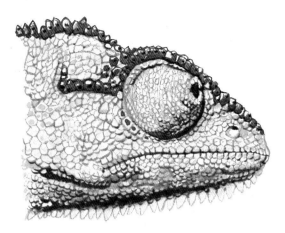

Mediterranean chameleon

Above: the chameleon's foot, with its fingers and strong claws that meet and match perfectly, forms a sort of pincers that enables the animal to maintain a firm grip on branches, with the help of its prehensile tail.
Top: the eyes of the chameleon (chameleonid saurian) are large bulbs protected by scaled eyelids with a small hole opening onto the iris at the center. They are independent and each of them can explore a different area.

To find food, the chameleon lurks among the branches, where it lies in wait, quite still, blending perfectly into the environment.
When an insect comes within range, the chameleon catches it with its tongue without moving. The tongue is very flexible, large at the top, like a club, moistened with a viscous substance, and very long; in some species, the tongue is as long as the creature's body.

21. THE CHAMELEON AND THE GILA MONSTER
(Squamate Diapsids, Saurians)

THE CHAMELEON

The chameleon is a very well-known creature because of its strange appearance, and for its ability — somewhat mythical — to change color. The chameleonid family (the scientific word means "little lion" or "lion camel") seems to derive from agamids, and is distributed in the warm, temperate regions of Asia, Africa, and southern Europe.

The chameleon's lifestyle is very monotonous. In general, it rarely climbs out of its habitat, trees or shrubs. In the morning, it simply leaves its shelter and nonchalantly seeks some branch on which it can bask in the sun. Its movement on branches is extremely slow and swaying like that of a leaf blown gently by the wind. Its feet have digits fused in opposal bunches of two and three, so that it can take a firm grip on the branch it is walking on. The chameleon's tail is prehensile too, which is unique among the saurians. The tail is used as a fifth limb.

HUNTING

When the sun has warmed it up, the reptile starts to hunt. Insects are its favorite food, and it loves locusts. To catch its prey, the chameleon stealthily approaches it and shoots out its very long, sticky tongue with incredible rapidity. If the insect is merely touched by the enlarged tip of the chameleon's tongue, it is infallibly caught, and swept into the reptile's enormous mouth. The tongue movement is so swift as to be practically invisible to the human eye; only in slow-motion pictures is it possible to observe the mechanics and precision of this impressive weapon, which fully compensates for the animal's slow movements.

But when the chameleon turns from hunter into prey (snakes are among its most feared enemies), then it is not so fortunate. Its slow movements prevent it from escaping; all it can do is let itself drop from the branch, and hope for the best.

THE EYES

The chameleon has strange, large, protruding eyes, which are moved independently to spot food or watch for the arrival of an enemy. They play an important role in hunting. Only when the unfortunate insect is within range do both eyes converge on it, probably to calculate the distance and position of the victim, and to aim correctly.

CHANGING COLOR

The chameleon's fame is also linked to its ability to change color whenever it wants, in order to adapt its appearance to that of the environment. Chameleons are not the only creatures that can do this; we also see it in many other saurians, but the show is not as spectacular. In chameleons, color is not used merely for camouflage; it also shows what sort of mood they are in. An irritated chameleon, or a chameleon trying

Beaded
lizard

Gila
monster

Above and left: the *Helodermatidae* live in North America, in the desert territories from Nevada to Mexico.
They are poisonous, and move about especially during the night or when darkness falls,
while they spend the daytime in underground holes.
During their long fasting periods, they live on the fat supplies accumulated in their tails.

THE GILA MONSTER AND THE BEADED LIZARD

The saurian *Helodermatidae* family — the escorpion or beaded lizard and the gila monster — can go without food and water for very long periods, for years sometimes, which makes areas where water and potential prey are scarce ideal habitats for it. It lives in the arid, desert territories of Mexico and Arizona.

The gila monster and the beaded lizard are the only poisonous saurians. The poison is produced by a specialized gland and is mixed with the saliva. But it is not injected into the victim's flesh through the teeth — the method snakes prefer (Chapter 24). The technique is much more rudimentary and primitive: the animal seizes its prey and holds it in its fangs for several minutes while the poisonous saliva spreads out over the victim's body. The method is obviously not very efficient, but we have to bear in mind that this animal only bites in extreme cases, and never when it is getting food. This saurian, in fact, feeds on eggs or small prey that it captures and swallows whole. It bites ferociously only when attacked, or if it feels threatened and unable to escape. When it is obliged to defend itself, the usually slow and lazy gila monster flashes its sharp teeth, and plunges them into its foe's body. It has a very strong hold: you can pull it, or beat it, but the saurian will not open its mouth. You can even cut it to pieces, but the head will remain firmly sunk in the victim's flesh, and the mouth can be forced open only with a knife. The creature is not excessively dangerous to man: only a dozen or so lethal cases have been reported, but the bite of this animal is exceptionally painful, and the wound swells a lot.

to defend its territory from a rival, does not bother to camouflage itself very much at all. Disease and illness also affect the creature's color, some species becoming deep black, and others an almost pure white, but the individual species have a far more restricted color range.

Desert monitor

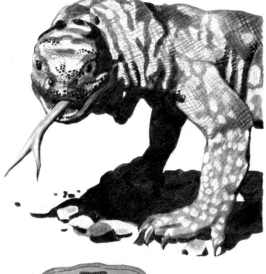

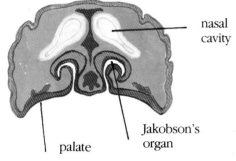

nasal cavity

Jakobson's organ

palate

The monitors (varanid saurians) have forked tongues that are only used for picking up odors from the ground.
Above: cross section of a monitor's maw.
The animal's Jacobson's organ evaluates the odors received by the tongue.

22. MONITORS AND LIZARDS

(Squamate Diapsids, Saurians)

MONITORS

The family name of this group of saurians, *Varanus*, may well derive from the Arabic "uran," meaning "lizard," because they are generally similar to common lizards in appearance. Their sizes are very different, however, with some species measuring 8 inches (20 centimeters), and others that are 12 feet (3.5 meters) long. They live in Asia, Africa, and Australia. Generally carnivorous and active hunters, they seek their prey with the help of a particularly sensitive olfactory system, and their long, forked tongues. This kind of tongue, which lizards and snakes have as well, is used to pick up odorous particles from the ground; it is then drawn back into the mouth, where the two small palate cavities, representing Jacobson's organ (see Chapter 23), perceive the smell. So all the monitor has to do when hunting is follow the odor its prey leaves behind, sticking out its tongue every now and again to make sure it is on the right track. The monitor's voracity is incredible: the animals can devour and swallow their own weight in flesh. After banquets such as these, however, they must lie down and digest. Sometimes they even sleep for as many as six days in a row.

Komodo dragon

The Komodo dragon lives in Komodo, one of the Lesser Sunda Islands in Indonesia. Only a few hundred specimens survive, mainly because man hunts the animals it feeds on: hog deer and wild pigs. Because of its shape and size, the Komodo dragon often acts as a dinosaur in popular documentary films.

The largest species of the family — and of all the lizards — is the Komodo dragon, once widespread in the Indonesian islands. This giant, over 10 feet (3 meters) long and weighing more than 220 pounds (100 kilograms), is an implacable hunter. It finds no difficulty in attacking animals bigger than itself, such as deer and horses, confronting them with courage — or recklessness. Since it is not poisonous, it rarely succeeds in killing its victims outright. When the prey, seriously wounded, crawls away and dies, the monitor uses its efficient olfactory system to find the carrion, but the smell of the decomposing body attracts the creature's mates, too. The Komodo dragon uses an unusual technique for eating the meat: it takes a deep bite, and then jumps backward, tearing the scrap away and swallowing it without further ado. Komodo dragons have run the risk of becoming extinct

The symbol of the National Park of Indonesia, set up to protect the Komodo dragon.

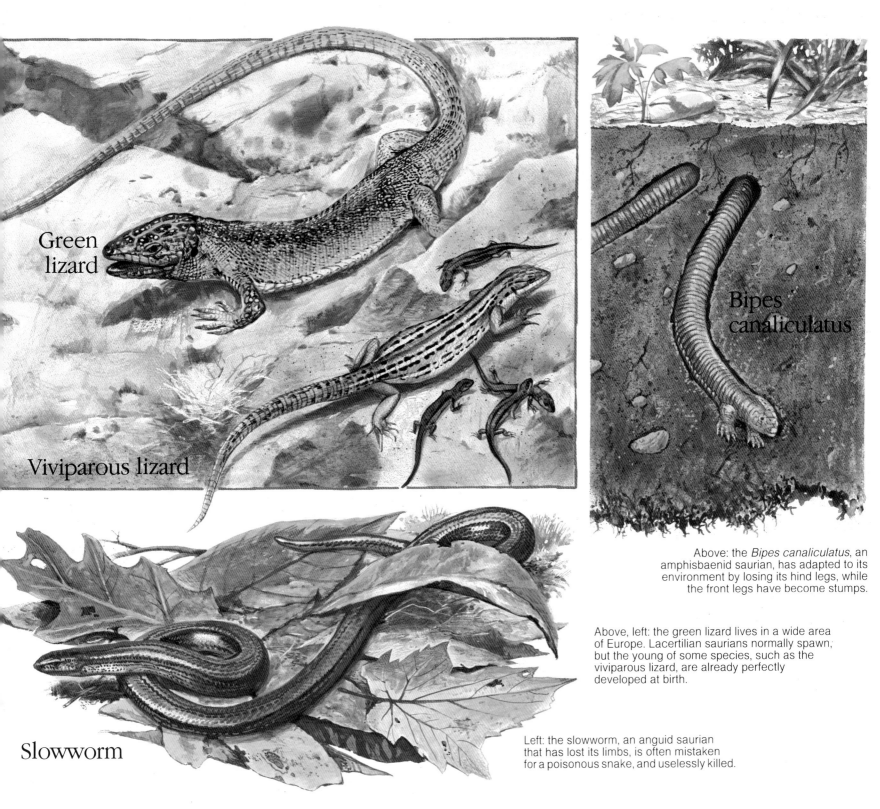

Green
lizard

Viviparous lizard

Slowworm

Bipes
canaliculatus

Above: the *Bipes canaliculatus*, an
amphisbaenid saurian, has adapted to its
environment by losing its hind legs, while
the front legs have become stumps.

Above, left: the green lizard lives in a wide area
of Europe. Lacertilian saurians normally spawn,
but the young of some species, such as the
viviparous lizard, are already perfectly
developed at birth.

Left: the slowworm, an anguid saurian
that has lost its limbs, is often mistaken
for a poisonous snake, and uselessly killed.

because they are hunted for their prized skins. Today, however, reservations have been set up to protect the survivors. It would indeed be unforgivable if we lost these enormous creatures forever. The monitor may not be nearly as nice as the panda, but it is unique.

LIZARDS

Lacertilians, better known as lizards, are the most common saurians. They are found in Asia, Africa, and Europe. One species, the common or viviparous lizard, lives in cold territories, as far north as Arctic Circle, and can even be found at an altitude of 8,000 feet (2,500 meters). The female of the species keeps the eggs warm in her body until the embryos are fully developed. Lacertilians too have a forked tongue that picks up odorous particles.

The colors of these animals are extremely varied. Generally speaking, the hues are bright and vivid. The

Lacerta viridis, the common green lizard, for example, is an almost fluorescent green with a blue hue. Needless to say, this is certainly not meant to let the creature blend in with the natural green of plants.

Lizards, like other saurians, can lose their tails, which is, oddly enough, a defensive stratagem. In one precise point of the tail vertebrae, the lizard can deliberately cause the tail to break away from its body. The tail stays alive and kicking, thrashing around for a few minutes, distracting and upsetting the foe, during which time the lizard will flee. The lost tail will grow again, but it will not be quite as good as the one that saved the lizard's life.

THE SLOWWORM

The *Anguidae* group of saurians includes species with snakelike bodies; in Latin, in fact, "anguis" means "snake." Some of them do have limbs, though, but

they are normally small or no more than stumps. The slowworm, the most classic representative of the *Anguidae*, has snakelike behavior, and is often taken for a snake and wrongly considered poisonous.

AMPHISBAENIDAE

These saurians live a subterranean life. They have segmented bodies, and the behavior patterns of the earthworm. The peculiar lifestyle of both creatures has given them very similar functional organizations, but their habits have practically nothing in common. *Amphisbaenidae* rarely leave their tunnels. Sometimes, but only at night, they do pop up to the surface. The rest of their life is played out in the dark of their shelters, where they are greatly helped by the specialization of their hearing system, a fundamental sense organ for all the *Amphisbaenidae*.

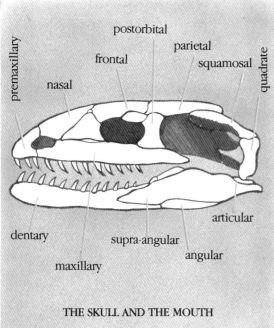

premaxillary
nasal
frontal
postorbital
parietal
squamosal
quadrate
dentary
supra-angular
maxillary
angular
articular

THE SKULL AND THE MOUTH

The ophidian skull is a diapsid model that is radically modified to give the animal an enormous mouth opening.

Snakes, in fact, are the only reptiles that are able both to lower the mandible, as we do, and to raise the upper jaw as well. Among the vertebrates, sharks and birds of prey can do this, but they use different mechanisms.

23. SNAKES: GENERAL FEATURES
(Squamate Diapsids, Ophidians)

Above: snakes first appeared at the time when the giant dinosaurs ruled over the Earth. They often ran the risk of being killed by the dinosaurs' huge feet. This may explain the strange evolution of their ears.

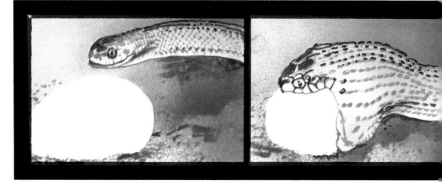

Like all other animals with snakelike bodies, ophidians, or snakes, had ancestors with legs, which were then lost in the course of further evolution; only in boas are there still traces of the thigh bone and pelvis. Snakes are scattered over all the five continents, so we may presume they appeared on Earth when its landmass was one single super-continent. After the continents broke away from one another, snakes proceeded with their evolution autonomously in different territories; but, as with the saurians, there is a considerable affinity among the species of the Eurasian, African, and Australian blocs on one side, and the North and South American ones on the other.

THE SKULL

Snakes too belong to the great diapsid group, but the two temporal openings (Chapter 5) are no longer visibile because of radical changes in the skull, which has much smaller side walls.

All the ophidians can open their mouths enormously wide to swallow down prey larger than themselves. One feature that enables them to do this is the flexibility and elasticity of their pharynxes; another is the fact that when they open their mouths, they raise the upper jaw too, while lowering and widening the two mandible bones. A python, for instance, whose head is no wider than a man's hand, is quite capable of swallowing a little pig or goat.

DIMENSIONS AND ANATOMY

The ophidian's elongated body comes in various sizes. The *Typhlopidae*, or blind snakes, are about 4 inches (10 centimeters) long, and just over half an inch (1.5 centimeters) in diameter.

Anaconda, on the other hand, can be more than 32 feet (10 meters) long, and a foot (30 centimeters) thick. Becoming a snake also meant great changes for the double organs inside the body: there is only one real lung, the right, that is as long and slender as the body itself; while the left lung is small, or even atrophied. A snake has two elongated kidneys, placed one after the other in a row. The spine also changed: all the vertebrae, apart from the first ones, bear arched ribs, which are free underneath the body, for there is no breastbone. Ribs can be raised or lowered, and play very important role in the serpentine movements.

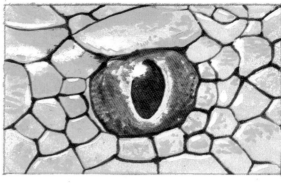

Top: a snake's lidless eye. Above:
a snake's eye just before sloughing.

Left: like the varanids, snakes have forked tongues
that pick up odors from the ground.
Diagram of the spine of a snake (in pink).

Snakes can open
their mouths
enormously wide to
swallow animals
that are larger than
themselves. The
egg-eating snake
swallows birds'
eggs and spits out
the broken shells
later.

SMELL THROUGH JACOBSON'S ORGAN

We have already seen this phenomenon in certain saurians: in the palate of every ophidian there are two little pits, called *Jacobson's organ,* lined with a very sensitive olfactory tissue.

While it moves, the snake repeatedly sticks its long, thin, forked tongue out to pick up odorous particles from the ground.

When the tongue is drawn back into the mouth, its two tips slip into the two pits of Jacobson's organ. It is their job to evaluate the chemical information contained in the particles.

This sense organ is very efficient and is used above all in hunting. There are no herbivorous snakes; they must all catch prey in order to survive.

A CONSTANTLY WATCHFUL EYE

Snakes are endowed with good sight but they lack eyelids, so their eyes are always open, even during sleep. However, their eyes are protected by a thin, usually transparent skin, with a veil of lachrymal liquid (tears) underneath. Ophidians, like saurians, slough: they cast off their skins when they have become too tight. Often, the whole horny shroud is shed in one piece, like a dress taken off and thrown on the floor. The snake makes the operation easier in the sloughing season by scraping itself against trees or rocks, or squeezing its way into narrow cracks. When the snake is changing its skin, as it were, its eyecovers become opaque, because they too will be shed. During this period, the creature must feel like it is looking through a sheet of frosted glass.

A DEAF EAR

Having no tympanic membrane and no eustachian tube, snakes perceive no sound at all; their deafness is not due to any atrophy of the sense organ, however, but because this organ has become extremely specialized in another direction. The columella, the little bone that transmits tympanic vibrations to the inner ear, is connected to the lower jawbone, and transmits its vibrations.

When the reptile is curled up, it always lays its head (and its jaw, too) on the ground, and any vibration is instantly transmitted to the ear and brain. But snakes do not use their ears for hunting, because their prey are usually too small to produce any vibrations whatsoever in the ground as they move.

This rather original sense organ — which all ophidians have — probably evolved to give snakes some defense against being trampled under the enormous feet of the numerous gigantic dinosaurs that populated the Earth at the beginning of the ophidians' evolution. Generally speaking, snakes are not aggressive: they bite only if disturbed, or when they have no chance of escaping.

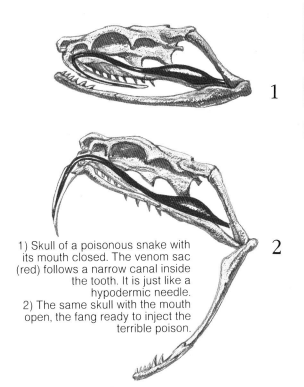

1) Skull of a poisonous snake with its mouth closed. The venom sac (red) follows a narrow canal inside the tooth. It is just like a hypodermic needle.
2) The same skull with the mouth open, the fang ready to inject the terrible poison.

24. VIPERS AND RATTLESNAKES
(Squamate Diapsids, Ophidians)

Rhinoceros viper

The rhinoceros viper owes its name to the small pointed horns on its nostrils.

Common viper

Asp viper

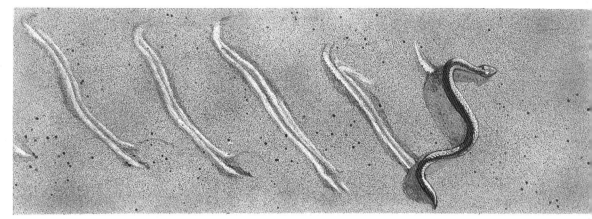

Above: when crotalids and viperids that live in the desert move on the hot sand, they only touch the ground with two points of the body to avoid being burned. They leave very typical tracks.
Top: viperids usually have stumpy bodies and short tails. The patterns on their skins, though they differ from one another, are a means of camouflage.

POISONOUS FANGS AND HUNTING

With the ophidians, too, we can only discuss a few of the various species that make up this enormous suborder. The *Viperidae* and *Crotalidae* represent the most evolved species of reptiles. The two families include extremely poisonous species whose apparatus for injecting venom is absolutely perfect.

In the short, stumpy maxillary bone are two long, pointed fangs with internal canals through which the poison produced by the venom glands flows. The canals open near the tips of the fangs. When the snake's mouth is closed, the fangs are folded inward; but when the snake opens it wide, they are raised by a series of bony levers. Generally speaking, snakes do not really bite; they plunge their teeth deep into the victim's flesh, with a downward movement, and inject their venom at the same time. The system works something like a hypodermic syringe.

This excellent weapon is mainly used for hunting, and the viper and rattlesnake families all follow the same rites. When the prey is within range, the snake darts its head and the front part of its body forward like lightning, injects poison into the victim's body, and then withdraws, just as swiftly, leaving the prey where it is. The movement is so quick that sometimes you cannot see it; many are the people who will tell how, during a walk or excursion, they suddenly felt a sharp pain in the calf, and realized only later that they had been bitten by a viper. After the attack, the snake waits patiently for the poison to take effect, and finally starts its search for the body, depending solely on the odorous traces picked up by its forked tongue.

THE *VIPERIDAE*

This family is found only in Asia, Europe, and Africa. We can therefore safely assume that it appeared on the Earth when North and South America and Australia had already broken away from the original continental mass. The favorite prey of vipers are small and large rodents. They should therefore be counted among the animals that are useful to man, but since they are truly dangerous, they are best killed on sight. *Viperidae* and *Crotalidae* leave their hideouts when the environmental temperature is between 15 and 30 degrees centigrade (60-85 Fahrenheit), so you can come across them both at night and during the day; it depends exclusively on the temperature. Like all snakes, vipers lay their eggs and simply leave them to their fate. But they differ from other snakes in that, when the eggs are laid, they already contain fully developed embryos, which can break the shells and emerge after only a few hours. In some species, the development of the embryo goes on inside the mother's body, and the female bears little vipers that already have their venom, and immediately go off hunting.

The most widespread species is the common viper, also called the adder, which lives in Europe and Asia. One of the most beautiful species due to the bright colors of its skin is the rhinoceros viper.

The crotalid's heat-sensitive organs, with their many tiny nerve endings, explore the environment to perceive any heat given out by warm-blooded prey, such as birds and mammals.

heat-sensitive organ

Western diamondback rattlesnake

Laboratory experiment to verify the function of the heat-sensitive organs: the rattlesnake attacks any heat source, even a lighted bulb.

Rattlesnakes have horny rings at the end of their tails, formed by the remains of successive sloughings. When shaken rapidly, the rings hit one another and produce an unmistakable sound that can be heard at distances of over 100 feet (30 meters).

THE *CROTALIDAE*

If America is lucky not to have the extremely dangerous vipers, it has the no less dangerous rattlesnake. The *Crotalidae* are in fact even more frightening than vipers because they are larger: the western diamondback rattlesnake is almost 10 feet (3 meters) long, the bushmaster almost 13 feet (4 meters). In a sense, however, rattlesnakes are less dangerous because they give man fair warning when they are about to attack. The tip of the creature's tail is fitted with a kind of rattle made of horny rings that releases a characteristic sound when the tail vibrates. In all, this proves that snakes are not naturally aggressive, unless, of course, they are hunting. When the rattlesnake sees a stranger approaching — one that is not on the menu — it frantically shakes its tail, as if to warn of its presence.

AN OUTSTANDING ORGAN

Rattlesnakes have an outstanding sense organ, unique among snakes. On both sides of their heads, between the nostrils and the eyes, they have two openings connected with two small chambers, each divided in half by a membrane. These are the heat-sensitive organs, which, as the term suggests, pick up the infrared rays released by a warm body. The snakes use them for hunting, letting themselves be steered toward the prey — a mouse, say — by the heat the tiny mammal releases. These so-called "heat receptors" enable the snake to hunt in any environmental situation: by day, at night, or in the dark dens of rodents. They can also be used to track birds and mammals with bodies warmer than the environment; but they do not work with cold-blooded prey such as amphibians and other reptiles. The importance of these organs can be demonstrated by placing a lighted bulb in front of a rattlesnake. Although the shape in no way resembles any kind of prey, although it gives off no odor, the rattlesnake perceives the heat and throws itself on the bulb.

King cobra

The angry Indian, or spectacled, or hooded cobra lifts its head and spreads its skin, which is normally folded neatly at the sides of the nape. A sort of hood is formed, with a pattern that resembles a pair of spectacles. Though they are very dangerous, cobras are tamed by snake charmers, who keep a safe distance from the animal. Cobras are deaf, and when they seem to dance to music in their rush baskets, they are really only following the slow movements of the instrument and the player's head with their eyes.

Laticauda laticaudata

Sea snakes are not the legendary monsters we read of in fairy tales, but poisonous reptiles up to 10 feet (3 meters) long that live in the warm coastal waters of the Pacific and Indian oceans. Some species have blackish crossbars on their skin, are very good swimmers, and hunt mostly eels, which they strike dead by injecting their deadly poison. When they plunge into the water, their nostrils are closed by a special valve.

Indian cobra

In India, snake charmers breed mongooses for cobra fighting. The common belief that these mammals are immune to poison is false: their quick reflexes and nimbleness, together with their thick fur, are the main weapons they use against their enemies.

Mongoose

25. COBRAS, SEA SNAKES, BOAS, AND PYTHONS
(Squamate Diapsids, Ophidians)

THE *ELAPIDAE*

The members of the *Elapidae* family are very poisonous snakes, widespread in all the five continents except Europe. Among the best-known are the cobra from Southeast Asia, the African mamba, and the American coral snakes. Their venomous fangs are much shorter than the vipers', and they do not fold inward. They are slender and sometimes very brightly colored creatures.

COBRAS

This species is distinguished by its "hoods," two folds of skin on the sides of its head which are supported by elongated neck ribs. When it feels threatened, the cobra, which is not usually very aggressive, raises its head and spreads its hood, which is normally folded, so that it looks bigger, frightening the enemy away. The king cobra, common in India, Indochina, and China, grows to a length of 13 feet (4 meters). It is a giant among cobras; and since the quantity of injectable venom is proportionate to the size of the snake, you can imagine how dangerous it is. Just a few drops of its poison can kill a horse in minutes. The spectacled cobra, very numerous in Southeast Asia, has a round hood, the dorsal scales of which bear typical spectacle-shaped markings. It lives everywhere,

even in gardens in large towns, and is the favorite partner of snake charmers. Among the various African cobras, the *Hemachatus,* or spitting cobra, has a rather peculiar defensive technique, which it uses against its foes but not in hunting. The animal does not bite its victim, but spits poison at it from a distance. The reptile raises its head, opens its mouth wide, and ejects the venom, which shoots out of its fang horizontally. The jet can hit targets as far as 6 feet (2 meters) away, but the poison takes effect only on the mucosa. If the venom touches the eyes, it can cause temporary, or even permanent, blindness.

THE ENEMY

Poisonous snakes have a dangerous, implacable enemy: the mongoose. This little mammal will never

shrink from fighting any cobra, no matter how violent the battle becomes. Its strategy is to tire the snake; with a series of feints, it tempts the snake to attack repeatedly, but skillfully avoids its fangs. When the exhausted cobra can no longer keep its head erect, the mongoose seizes the nape of its neck, bites viciously, and kills it.

THE *HYDROPHIDAE*

The areas of the Pacific Ocean that face Africa, southern Asia, Australia, and Central America are populated by the *Hydrophidae,* or sea snakes, the only snakes that are adapted for a marine life. Their main feature is the paddlelike tail: when waved, it propels the animal through the water. They range in length from 3 feet (1 meter) or a little more, like the

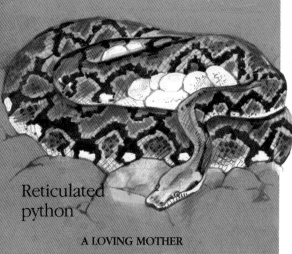

Anaconda

Boa constrictor

Reticulated python

The anaconda, up to 30 feet (9 meters) long, is the largest living reptile. It is common in South America, where it lives in rivers. The boa constrictor, up to 16 feet (5 meters) long, is a tree-dweller in Central and South America. Neither of these snakes is poisonous: they kill their prey simply by squeezing it in their powerful coils.

A LOVING MOTHER

Among *squamates*, only the female python looks after her eggs. She wraps her body around them, and sits on them for months at a time; in the reproduction period of the year, their body temperatures are higher.

common sea snake, to almost 10 feet (3 meters), like the *Hydrophis spiralis*. They use their potent poison to kill the fish they feed on, but they never attack man.

THE *BOIDAE*

This family is widespread in the Old and New Worlds. Pythons, including the reticulated or regal python, live in Africa, India, Indochina, and Australia. Boas, including the boa constrictor and the anaconda, live in Central and South America. Pythons lay their eggs while the female boas keep them in their bodies until the embryos are fully developed. These reptiles are hunted by man, both for their skin, which is used for making handbags, shoes, and other articles, and for their meat which the Chinese, for instance, find excellent. The *Boidae* family includes the largest snakes of the world, but it is difficult to say which one

holds the record: both reticulated pythons and anacondas almost 32 feet (10 meters) long have been found.

The *Boidae* have no poison glands, and their hunting technique is quite different from the ones we have encountered up to now. Many species, such as the boa constrictor, love to lie in wait in trees; others, such as the anaconda, prefer to lurk in the water, waiting for some thirsty, unsuspecting animal to come along. These two creatures are quite capable of waiting days, or even weeks, but sooner or later they will be rewarded. When a poor animal is within range, the snake attacks it, shooting its head forward and biting the prey at random. Immediately afterward, it coils its powerful body around the victim and squeezes. These reptiles can start swallowing their prey before the onset of death, and they begin with the head as usual.

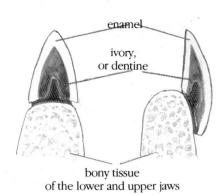

enamel

ivory, or dentine

bony tissue
of the lower and upper jaws

Before the thecondonts, teeth used to
simply lie on the bone, either on the top
(left) or on the inner surface (right).

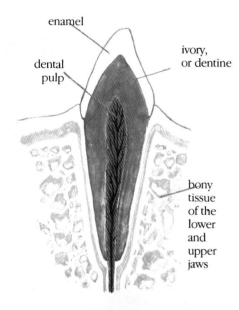

enamel

ivory, or dentine

dental pulp

bony tissue of the lower and upper jaws

The thecodonts' teeth were deeply
embedded in the bone, in a cavity
called the tooth socket.

Ornithosuchus

In the Triassic Period, around 200 million years ago, there lived the *Ornithosuchus*, the first
known specimen of the thecodont archosaur reptiles.

26. THE MAIN EVOLUTIONARY LINE OF REPTILES: DINOSAURS
(Diapsids, Thecodont Archosaurs)

One of the most important evolutionary lines of
vertebrates are the dinosaurs, also called "ruling
reptiles" because, unchallenged, they dominated the
Earth for more than a hundred million years during
the Secondary Era. We are all well acquainted with the
word dinosaur, but in the scientific classification of
reptiles, the term is not actually used to indicate
reptiles with diapsid skulls; that is, with two temporal
openings in the walls of the skull (Chapter 5).

TEETH

The most appropriate name for the great dinosaur
group is "thecodont archosaurs," because these
reptiles discovered a new way for linking the tooth to
the upper and lower jaws. Teeth are very ancient
structures: they first appeared in placoderms 400
million years ago (see the volume on marine life in
this series), and all the classes we have examined so

far had them: fish, amphibians, and reptiles. But we
have seen that teeth simply lay on the bone, and were
linked to it by bands of small connective fibers. Teeth
like that were not very stable, and could fall out easily;
but this was no problem, for there were a host of other
teeth ready and waiting to take their place, as still
occurs in sharks, for example. The thecodont
archosaurs changed all this: they invented a cavity, the
tooth socket in the maxillary bone, in which the tooth
is firmly embedded. Mammals, too, were to adopt this
system. Unlike mammals, however, the thecodonts
could change their teeth as often as necessary. All
fossil skeletons of dinosaurs still have their teeth.

ORIGINS

The most ancient thecodont archosaur we know is the
Ornithosuchus, which lived on the Earth more than
200 million years ago. A preliminary, brief examination
tends to reveal a fairly well-evolved creature, which

Throughout the Jurassic and Cretaceous periods, the thecodont archosaurs gave rise to various evolutionary lines, with a great number of specimens, especially dinosaurs; they later became extinct except for birds and crocodiles.

leads us to deduce that the origins of its evolutionary line date back to the Permian Period, 280 million years ago, with the most ancient reptiles, cotylosaurs (see Chapter 7). The *Ornithosuchus*, in fact, had already adopted the erect stature; it could walk on its hind limbs, which were much stronger and better developed than its forelimbs. Its long tail counterbalanced the weight of its body, which was bent forward as a result of the new way of locomotion. It is strange that while the first thecodont archosaurs stood up, other secondary branches deriving from them started to go on all fours again.

EXPANSION

Thecodont archosaurs proved to be exceptionally well adapted for life on dry land. We have already seen the numerous evolutionary lines of reptiles that moved into the water, and adapted to the new element (Chapters 15-17); but not the thecodont archosaurs, for they proceeded with a completely terrestrial existence.

Various orders in various periods derived from thecodont archosaurs: loricates, pterosaurs, ornithischians, saurischians, and indirectly, even a new class, birds.

Loricates appeared early on in the Triassic Period and their anatomical organization retained many primitive features which have come down to us more or less unchanged in today's crocodiles.

Pterosaurs, now extinct, appeared in the late Triassic Period and lived on during the whole Cretaceous Period. These reptiles were able to glide through the air — taking advantage of air currents — on their fragile wings, thin membranes of skin stretched between the forelimbs and the trunk.

Ornithischians and saurischians represent the famous group of dinosaurs, large and small, two- and fourfooted, herbivorous and carnivorous. The distinction between the two orders is exclusively based on the different structure of the pelvis, which in ornithischians was akin to that of birds, while in saurischians was typically reptilian. Dinosaurs, which appeared toward the middle of the Triassic Period, were destined for one of the most mysterious events in the history of vertebrates: their sudden mass extinction 65 million years ago, at the end of the Secondary Era.

In the Jurassic Period, true birds derived from the saurischian dinosaurs, creatures that were able to fly actively, thanks to the peculiar structure of their wings, which could "beat" the air without ripping.

Although it might seem paradoxical, birds are in fact the creatures most closely affiliated to the now-extinct dinosaurs.

The general features of all reptiles are found in crocodiles, and it is fitting that we should end this volume on the great class of reptiles with them.

Orthosuchus

The *Orthosuchus* was a protosuchian of the Triassic Period that lived in the South African wetlands.

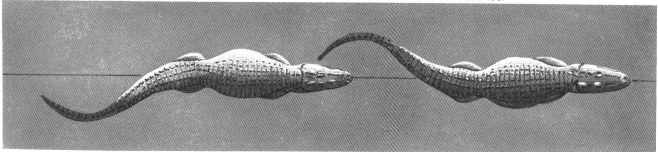

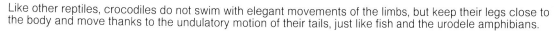

Like other reptiles, crocodiles do not swim with elegant movements of the limbs, but keep their legs close to the body and move thanks to the undulatory motion of their tails, just like fish and the urodele amphibians.

27. EXTINCT CROCODILES: GENERAL FEATURES

(Archosaurian Diapsids, Loricates)

Today, the only survivors of the great group of thecodont archosaurs are crocodiles, scientifically referred to as "loricates," from the Latin word *lorica*, a leather cuirass reinforced with metal sheets used in ancient Rome. The crocodile's back is, in fact, covered by strong, broad, horny scales supported by similar bony scales underneath.

PROTOSUCHIANS AND MESOSUCHIANS

Protosuchians were the first crocodiles that appeared on the Earth in the Triassic Period 200 million years ago. The anatomy of these distant forefathers makes

us think that they preferred dry land to the aquatic life. The *Orthosuchus*, for example, had limbs that it could lift from the ground when it wanted to move around at a fair pace. The preference for water shared by all species of loricates still living today became evident in the Jurassic Period, more than 150 million years ago. In that period, a group of crocodiles called mesosuchians — more evolved than the previous ones — swam in the seas of the Earth. The limbs of some of them, the *Metriorhyncus* and the *Geosaurus*, had turned into flippers. It is possible that they were no longer able to move on dry land, or if they could it was only very awkwardly and only to lay their eggs.

EUSUCHIANS

In the late Cretaceous Period, 65 million years ago, the mesosuchians disappeared and a third group of crocodiles — very akin to present-day ones — called eusuchians made its first appearance. At that time, the climate was still favorable for reptiles, so this evolutionary line soon spread, taking on gigantic sizes. In Texas, in the fossil layers of that period, a skull has been found of a specimen that must have been 52 feet (16 meters) long, as its head alone

measures 5 feet (1.5 meters); it is presumed to have been the largest crocodile that ever existed. With its enormous mouth, it could attack and tear contemporary, huge, herbivorous dinosaurs to pieces. Indeed, it might have been the very abundance of food supplies — for like crocodiles, the dinosaurs lived in ponds and marshes — that caused the advent of giantism. And huge crocodiles disappeared with the extinction of dinosaurs.

LIVING CROCODILES: ENVIRONMENT AND HABITS

Nowadays, apart from one species that likes brackish water, all loricates live in the fresh waters of the tropical regions; there are none in Europe, of course, where the climate is not suitable for crocodiles, but there once were, as numerous fossil finds prove. Crocodiles become active only when their body temperature reaches 30-32 degrees centigrade (90-95 Fahrenheit). This is one of the reasons for their lazy idling in the sun during the day, while they start hunting at sunset, always in the water where they spend the night, too. They are excellent, fast swimmers, thanks to the thrust provided by their

Geosaurus

Metriorhynchus

Thanks to the special conformation of their palates, loricates can lie in wait leaving only their eyes and nostrils peeping out of the water.

Left: the mesosuchians are a more advanced line of loricates. During the Jurassic Period, they were already perfectly adapted to life in the sea. In the foreground we see two *Metriorhynchi*, with armored bodies and limbs that have turned into flippers. In the background is a *Geosaurus*, with a longer shape and without any armor at all.

only their nostrils peeping out, and lie there, in a sort of estivation, during which all their vital functions slow down remarkably. They can remain in these pratically lifeless conditions for weeks, but become perfectly active again when there is enough water.

REPRODUCTION

Loricates reproduce by means of eggs that are laid on land, usually in nests of mud and decaying leaves that ferment and engender the warmth needed for the embryo to develop.

Crocodiles — unique among the living reptiles — are very scrupulous about looking after their offspring. The female Nile crocodile never leaves her nest while the eggs are developing; she stays there to protect them against the multitude of predators. That is not all: when the moment comes for the eggs to hatch, she delicately breaks the shells, using her huge mouth, and helps the newborns to emerge. Immediately afterward, she picks them up in her mouth a few at a time, and takes them into the water. A few trips to and fro, and the whole brood is safe, and the young can already start searching for food on their own. But it is a couple of weeks before they have the courage to stray far from their mother, for they are used to her taking them in her mouth at the first sign of danger. When young, crocodiles have many enemies, but as time passes, they grow bigger, and soon lose all their enemies, save one: man.

THEY NEED PROTECTION

Man has hunted crocodiles for their valuable skin so much that the number of specimens of all species has greatly declined. The risk of extinction increases day by day, partly because of the insensitive disregard for the need to protect these ungraceful and much feared animals.

Many female crocodiles protect their young by keeping them inside their mouths.

powerful tails. Moreover, unlike the other reptiles, they have a rather peculiar feature, one that is typical of mammals, man included: a hard palate, and a valve system in the nostrils and throat that enables them to breathe with their mouths open in the water, as long as their nostrils are above the surface.

All are carnivorous, and have no particular preferences; they will attack any other reptile, bird, or mammal, and man, too. Crocodiles are frightening hunters that use a very simple method. From the water, they slowly explore the shores and riverbanks, letting only the top of their head poke through to the surface; we are all familiar with adventure films in which a floating log suddenly becomes a horrible grinning crocodile. Once it has spotted the prey, the crocodile cautiously approaches it, and clamps it in its mouth, even if the victim is larger than itself. The prey is swept down deep into the water and drowns. Since their teeth are not suitable for ripping or chewing flesh, crocodiles let their victims putrefy under water, before dismembering them by thrusting their teeth in, clamping their jaws tight, and threshing their heads around until the piece comes away.

If water becomes scarce, or the river dries up, crocodiles let themselves sink into the mud, leaving

Common Nile crocodile

Spur-winged plover

Crocodile bird

head of a Crocodile

28. THE CROCODILE, THE ALLIGATOR, THE GAVIAL

(Archosaurian Diapsids, Loricates)

Crocodilia, Alligatoridae, and *Gavialidae* are the three loricate families living today. With exception of the very long-snouted gavial, there are not many differences among them except the shape and layout of their teeth, and features of the horny shields of their bodies and heads, which the gavials do not always have.

CROCODILIA

This is the best-known family; indeed, all the loricates are often called crocodiles. Crocodiles were known in ancient times. The Egyptians used to depict them in their sculptures, and worship them so fervently that they even embalmed them. The family is very widely

Some species of birds look after cleaning the crocodile's skin and teeth, while seeking parasites or remains of food. The reptile loves to keep its maw wide open in the sunshine, patiently waiting for the bird to finish its job.

distributed in Central America, Africa, India, and Australia. The Nile crocodile, the best known, reaches lengths of some 23 feet (7 meters). Once, it could be found in all the rivers of Africa, the Nile included, but its habitat is much more restricted nowadays.

Young crocodiles are dark green, but as the years go by, their skin tends to become covered with deposits and debris of various kinds. Sometimes, even little water plants take root on it and help to camouflage the animal, which really does tend to look like an old tree trunk in its less active moments. These crocodiles sometimes dig tunnels underwater that lead to rooms where the animals can hide away and enjoy their meals.

A SEA CROCODILE

The *Crocodilia* family also includes the only species that ventures into the open sea as well, far away from the coasts: the saltwater crocodile, which usually lives in river estauries. As it lives in this environment, it feeds on food that is extremely rich in salt, which it

then eliminates through tears produced by special glands. This is probably where the expression "crocodile tears" comes from.

ALLIGATORIDAE

In America and in the Yangtze River in China there lives another loricate family, the *Alligatoridae.* Once, large herds of alligators could be seen basking in the sun on the banks of lazy muddy or sandy rivers; it was even possible to approach them, because they were not very aggressive. But after years of extensive slaughter for commercial purposes, the alligators have now turned into shy, wary animals that take to the water at the slightest sign of danger. Because of the quality and value of their skins, they are often bred in special centers, where they grow very rapidly: in one year, an alligator 15 inches (40 centimeters) long can grow to a length of 6½ feet (2 meters), which is a marketable size. Among the best-known species in this family, are the American alligator, which lives in the southeastern United States and reaches a length of

American alligator

Gavials feed exclusively on fish that they skillfully catch with their slender maws.

True gavial

head of an Alligator

head of a Gavial

Above, left: like crocodiles, alligators live an amphibian life; they idle about outside the water, and hunt their prey in it.

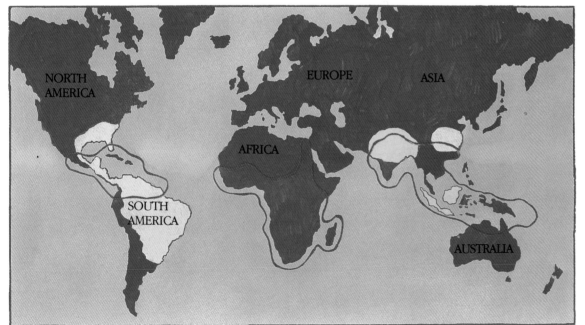

NORTH AMERICA

EUROPE

ASIA

AFRICA

SOUTH AMERICA

AUSTRALIA

Distribution of the three loricate families. Crocodiles: red-bordered area.
Alligators: yellow-bordered area. Gavials: green-bordered area.

19 feet (6 meters); and the smaller Cayman, which inhabits Central and South America and grows to a length of 5 feet (1.5 meters).

GAVIALIDAE

Nowadays, this family, very common in India and Indonesia, consists of one single species, *Gavialis gangeticus*, or true gavial. They are easily distinguished from other crocodiles because of their very long snouts and their multitude of teeth. Their length is very respectable, up to 23 feet (7 meters); their shy nature, and their diet — nothing but fish — make them quite inoffensive to man and to other animals. The gavial too is hunted; not for its skin, but because of the damage it causes to fish. It is not only good at fishing, but is also an insatiable eater.

Class	Subclass
	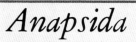 *Anapsida*
	Parapsida
	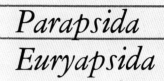 *Euryapsida*
	Synapsida
Reptiles	*Diapsida*

Fossil of *Askeptosaurus*, a crocodilelike eosuchian, 6.5 feet (2 meters) long, that adjusted to life in aquatic habitats and lived in the Triassic Period. It was found near Varese in Lombardy, northern Italy.

Living suborders are underlined. Numbers after names refer to chapters in this volume.

Classification of living and extinct reptiles.

Fossil of *Ichthyosaurus crassicostatus*, a dolphinlike ichthyosaur that lived in the seas of the Jurassic Period, around 180 million years ago. Among the ribs of this female specimen, found at Holzmaden in West Germany, there are the traces of the young that were to be born; another of the young can be seen on the right.